PHILIPPIANS
AND COLOSSIANS

H. A. IRONSIDE

An Ironside Expository Commentary

PHILIPPIANS
AND COLOSSIANS

H. A. IRONSIDE

Kregel
Academic & Professional

Philippians and Colossians: An Ironside Expository Commentary

Originally published in 1920. Reprinted in 2007 by Kregel Publications, a division of Kregel, Inc., 2450 Oak Industrial Dr. NE, Grand Rapids, MI 49505.

ISBN 978-0-8254-2920-0

Printed in the United States of America

2 3 4 5 6 / 18 17 16 15 14

CONTENTS

5

COLOSSIANS

PHILIPPIANS

PREFACE

These notes have been jotted down at odd times, over a period of nearly two years, while the writer has been busily engaged in gospel work. They pretend to no literary value, and repetitions may sometimes occur. But such as they are, they are sent forth with the earnest hope that they may be blessed to some of "the quiet in the land" who enjoy simple things, plainly put.

—H. A. IRONSIDE

Introductory Thoughts

The account of the labors and sufferings of the apostle Paul and his companions in Philippi is given in the sixteenth chapter of the Acts. They went to Macedonia in response to the vision of a man of that country calling for help, which Paul had seen at Troas. But when they reached the capital, there was apparently no such man feeling his need and awaiting them. Instead, they came first in touch with a few women who were accustomed to gather for prayer in a quiet place by the riverside outside the city. There the Lord opened Lydia's heart to attend to the things spoken by Paul. Others too were evidently reached, among them some brethren as verse 40 makes clear. But it was when cast into prison that the greatest work was done. The jailer and his household were won for Christ before the messengers of God's grace took their departure for Thessalonica.

The infant church was very dear to the heart of the apostle, and he was very dear to them. Their love and care were shown after he left them, at various times, and, one would judge, for a number of years. But at last they lost touch with him, apparently during his imprisonment at Caesarea. It was when he was in Rome that they again got into communication with him and, fearing he might be in need, sent him an expression of their love and care by the hand of a trusted and beloved brother who was one of themselves, Epaphroditus. Having fulfilled his ministry, this faithful man fell sick, and his illness was of sufficient duration for word regarding it to reach Philippi, and the news of the anxiety of the saints there concerning him had come back to Rome about the time that he became convalescent. Deciding at once to return, he was entrusted with the letter we have before us, which was, one would judge, dictated to him by the apostle.

It is an epistle of joy, a letter of cheer. On the other hand, it contains needful exhortation for a wilderness people, liable to fall out by the way.

It would seem that Epaphroditus had communicated to Paul a certain concern that was weighing upon his heart regarding a misunderstanding or a positive quarrel between two women in the assembly—both much esteemed by the saints and by the apostle himself—which if not checked and healed, was likely to prove a source of sadness, and possibly even division in days to come.

This appears to be much in the apostle's mind as he indites his epistle. He seeks so to present Christ that the hearts of all may be ravished with Him, and thus all selfish aims disappear, and all that is of the flesh be judged in His presence.

This is ever what is needed when the flesh is at work among believers. Therefore the great importance of this portion of the Word of God in the present hour of the church's history.

The epistle falls very naturally into four divisions, and these are rightly indicated in our common version by the four chapters. The theme of the whole might be put in the three words, *"Christ is all!"* It is the epistle of Christ. It occupies us with Himself; and each separate division presents Him in some different way, and indicates the subjective result in the believer as he is occupied with Christ objectively in the manner presented.

Chapter 1 sets forth Christ as our *life*, and the evangelistic spirit or the gospel mind.

In chapter 2 we have Christ as our *example*, and the lowly mind or the humble spirit of those who would follow Him.

Chapter 3 gives us Christ as our *object*, and, subjectively, we have the steadfast spirit, the determined mind—that is, the heart and thoughts centered on Himself.

In the last chapter, Christ is set forth as our *strength and supply*, and naturally we have with this the confident mind, the spirit of trust that should characterize all who know the resources that are in Him.

It will be readily seen that the epistle is a very practical one. It has to do with our state rather than our standing, with responsibility rather than privilege, with communion rather than with union. In other words, it is an epistle suited to our wilderness journey. It was written to guide our feet while going through this world. It is a pastoral ministry of a very precious kind.

Others have written very fully and helpfully on this part of the Word of God, whose writings are readily obtainable. It is not the present writer's thought to attempt a labored exposition of the epistle, but simply to jot down some notes that embody the results of his own study, and which it is hoped may be used by the Holy Spirit for the edification and comfort of fellow saints, particularly such as are becoming discouraged because of the Way. Much has been gleaned from what others have set forth, and no pretension is made as to originality of treatment. If Christ Himself becomes a little more appreciated by a few of His own, the object in view will have been attained.

PART 1

CHRIST, THE BELIEVER'S LIFE, AND THE EVANGELISTIC SPIRIT

CHAPTER 1

SALUTATION

Philippians 1:1–2

Paul and Timotheus, the servants of Jesus Christ, to all the saints in Christ Jesus which are at Philippi, with the bishops and deacons: Grace be unto you, and peace, from God our Father, and from the Lord Jesus Christ. (vv. 1–2)

It is noticeable how, in many of his letters, the apostle links up younger and less experienced fellow laborers with himself, as here, in his salutations. He was an apostle by the Lord's call, occupying a unique place as His special messenger to the Gentiles. But he never stands aloof in complacent dignity apart from others who are engaged in the same ministry. He had taken Timothy with him when the latter had not long been in the knowledge and path of the truth, and he testifies later, in this same letter, of the truth that was in him. In his care for the development of the younger brethren, Paul becomes a model for older teachers and evangelists to the end of the dispensation. If others are to follow on in the ways that be in Christ, it is well that more experienced men take a personal interest in their less experienced brethren who manifest a measure of gift, and by associating them with themselves in ministry, lead and encourage them in the path of faith. It is often the other way, and the young are disheartened, and permitted to slip back into business pursuits, who, if wisely advised, and helped when needed, might become able ministers of the truth.

Paul and Timothy take no official title here. They are simply servants of Jesus Christ. The word means "bondmen." They were purchased servants, and as such, belonged entirely to Him whom they gladly owned as their Anointed Master. They were His by right, and they had renounced all title to do the will of the flesh. Nor is it only ministering brethren who are so designated in Scripture. This is the name that is used of all Christians. Though sons and heirs we are also bondmen of love, whose delight it should be to yield ourselves unto Him as those who are alive from the dead.

The saints as a whole at Philippi are greeted, and the elders and deacons specially mentioned. This is unusual. It evidently implies a particular sense of obligation to the elders and deacons on the part of the apostle, probably in connection with ministry of the assembly's gift of love. There may also be the thought of addressing the leaders, or guides, in a special way, in view of the "rift in the lute"—the unhappiness between Euodia and Syntyche, which he desired to rectify.

Elders may, or may not, be official. In the early church they were definitely appointed by apostolic authority. It may be unwise, and going beyond Scripture, for saints in feebleness today to set up or ordain official elders. On the other hand, those measurably possessing the qualifications indicated in the epistles to Timothy and Titus, should be recognized by fellow believers as God-appointed elders, whose counsel should be sought, and who are responsible to watch for souls and to take oversight in the house of God. To fail to own such would be insubjection to the Word of God, but a true bishop or overseer would be the last man to insist upon obedience to him. He would rather lead by serving the saints and by the force of a godly example.

Deacons are those who minister in temporal things and should be chosen by the saints for this purpose. The word means "servant" but is different to that used above. It is not "bondman" but a servant acting voluntarily, and in response generally to the expressed desire of others.

Notice the little word *all*. It is used very significantly in this epistle—in a way not found anywhere else in the writings of the apostle Paul.

Observe its use in verses 4, 7, 8, and 25 in this chapter, and verse 26 in chapter 2. Is it not plain that Paul desired to bind all together in one bundle of love in this way, refusing to even seem to recognize any incipient division among them? He greeted them all, he thought well of them all, he prayed for them all. He knew it would in the end be well with them all. And so he exhorted them all to stand fast in one spirit. As customary in all his letters, he wished them grace and peace. Grace was the general Grecian salutation. Peace was that of the Hebrew. So he links the two together. Grace in its highest sense, favor against desert, could only be known by the Christian. And true peace rests upon the work of the cross, whether it be that peace with God, which is fundamental, or the peace of God, which the apostle here would have the saints enter into and enjoy from day to day. Both descend from God, now revealed as Father, and from our Lord Jesus Christ, through whom we have been brought into this place of favor.

CHAPTER 2

The Introduction

Philippians 1:3–11

I thank my God upon every remembrance of you, always in every prayer
of mine for you all making request with joy, for your fellowship in the
gospel from the first day until now; being confident of this very thing,
that he which hath begun a good work in you will perform it until the
day of Jesus Christ: even as it is meet for me to think this of you all,
because I have you in my heart; inasmuch as both in my bonds, and
in the defence and confirmation of the gospel, ye all are partakers of
my grace. For God is my record, how greatly I long after you all in the
bowels [or, tenderness] of Jesus Christ. And this I pray, that your love
may abound yet more and more in knowledge and in all judgment [or,
perception]; that ye may approve things that are excellent; that ye may
be sincere and without offence [or, blameless] till the day of Christ.
Being filled with the fruits of righteousness, which are by Jesus Christ,
unto the glory and praise of God. (vv. 3–11)

In these verses we have the apostle's own introduction to this delightful speci-
men of early Christian correspondence. His interest in the saints at Philippi
did not cease with his leaving their city. Through all the years that had passed

he had borne them on his heart, and presented them to God in prayer. There were sweet and blessed memories too that filled him with gladness as he looked back on the season of ministry spent among them, and as he learned of their continuance in the grace of God in after days.

He thanks God upon every remembrance of them. There was nothing, apparently, in their past history that had caused him pain or anxiety of mind. And so, in every prayer of his for them all, he preferred his request with joy. Their fellowship with him in the gospel had been consistent from the beginning. It will be noticed what a large place "fellowship" has in this epistle, and also how frequently "the gospel" is mentioned. An assembly of saints walking together in the fear of the Lord, exercised about holding forth the Word of Life to the unsaved, is likely to know more of real fellowship than a company of believers occupied chiefly with their own affairs, their own blessings—all about themselves. On the other hand, no assembly can prosper that fails to recognize the importance of the divine and holy principles given in the Word to guide believers in this scene.

Fellowship in the gospel may be exercised in various ways: by prayer, by participation in the public testimony, by furnishing the means to enable the laborer to go forth unhindered by perplexities and anxieties as to necessary means to carry on his work. Every servant of Christ going forth for the Name's sake, "taking nothing of the Gentiles," should be entirely cast upon the Lord for his support. On the other hand, it should be esteemed a privilege on the part of those abiding at home, to help them by ministering in temporal things; and such ministry will never be forgotten by Him who has said, "[Whosoever] receiveth a prophet in the name of a prophet shall receive a prophet's reward."

I remember a brother's definition of fellowship. He was a teamster, and was asked, "What do you understand by fellowship?" He replied, "For each one to pull his own trace and keep it tight." The simile is a crude one, but will be readily understood.

It is noticeable that the apostle had no doubt as to the final outcome for every true believer. He was absolutely confident that the One who had begun a good work in them would never leave off until He had perfected that which He Himself had commenced. But this would only be attained and manifested in the day of Jesus Christ. A godly old brother used often to say, "The Lord always looks at His people as they will be when they are done." And it is well for us if we can learn to look at them in the same way.

An incident is told of an artist who had conceived in his mind a great picture, which he meant to be the masterpiece of his life. He was working on a large canvas, putting in the drabs and grays that were to compose the background, when a friend entered, unnoticed. The artist worked on with enthusiasm, not aware of the onlooker's presence. But, finally happening to turn, he saw him, and exclaimed, "What do you think of this? I intend it to be the greatest work I have ever done." His friend burst into a laugh and exclaimed, "Why, to be frank, I don't think much of it. It seems to me to be only a great daub." "Ah," replied the artist, at once sensing the situation, "you cannot see what is going to be there. I can."

And so it is with God our Father. He sees in every believer that which will be fully brought out at the judgment seat of Christ, and He is working now toward that end. We too often see the present imperfection and forget the future glory. But, in the day of Jesus Christ, when all shall be manifested, every believer will be conformed to the image of God's blessed Son. Surely we can join with the apostle even now and say, "It is meet for me to think this of you all." Thus to look upon God's people will deliver from much strife, and from disappointment, when we see crudities and carnalities in those from whom we had expected better things. It is humbling and healthful too to remember that others probably see similar imperfections in us.

Paul carried the saints in his heart, and, though himself in prison, he recognized their fellowship in the defense and confirmation of the gospel, and rejoiced in the manner in which they shared this grace with him. He calls God to witness how greatly he yearned after every one of them in the tender love of Christ Jesus; and in verses 9–11 we have his prayer, which reminds us somewhat of the prayer in Colossians 1. He would have their love abound yet more and more in knowledge and all perception, or discernment. Brotherly love is not a matter of mere sentimentality; it is love in the truth. And this calls for study of the Word of God in order that one may know just how to manifest that love according to each particular occasion. Let us remember there is never a time when we are not called upon to show love to our brother, but we cannot always manifest it in the same way, if subject to the Word of God. Therefore the need of instruction in that Word, and enlightenment by the Holy Spirit, that we may perceive what is in accordance with the mind of God.

The first clause in the tenth verse is sometimes rendered, "That ye may try the things that differ;" or, as given above, "Approve things that are excellent." The meaning is practically the same. For by testing things that differ, we approve what is excellent. Again the test is the Word of God. That Word is given to try all things, and it will manifest what is truly excellent, thus giving the believer to understand how he may walk so as to please God, that he may be sincere and blameless in the day of Christ.

Attention has often been called to the striking fact that we have here the anglicized Latin word *sincere*, meaning, literally, "without wax"—used to translate a Greek word meaning "sun-tested." It might seem at first as though there is no connection between the two terms. But we are told that the ancients had a very fine porcelain that was greatly valued and brought a very high price. This ware was so fragile that it was only with the greatest difficulty it could be fired without being cracked, and dishonest dealers were in the habit of filling in the cracks that appeared with a pearly-white wax, which looked enough like the true porcelain to pass without being readily detected in the shops. If held to the light, however, the wax was at once manifested as a dark seam, and honest Latin dealers marked their wares "sine cera" (without wax). Thus the apostle would have the saints tested by the sunlight of God's truth and holiness and found to be without wax, that is, he would have them straightforward, and honorable in all their dealings. Anything that savors of sham or hypocrisy is as the wax used to hide the imperfection in the porcelain.

Blameless (see also 2:15) refers to "motive" rather than to act, I take it. It is not the same thing as sinless, which would, of course, imply complete moral perfection. "Blamelessness" implies right motives. "The fruits of righteousness" of verse 11 is the same as in Hebrews 12:11, where "the peaceable fruit of righteousness" is the result of exercise under the hand of God. All is through Jesus Christ, unto the glory and praise of God.

CHAPTER 3

JOY IN GOSPEL TESTIMONY

Philippians 1:12–20

But I would ye should understand, brethren, that the things which happened unto me have fallen out rather unto the furtherance of the gospel; so that my bonds in Christ are manifest in all the palace [or, Praetorium, i.e., Caesar's Guard], and in all other places; and many of the brethren in the Lord, waxing confident by my bonds, are much more bold to speak the word without fear. Some indeed preach Christ even of envy and strife; and some also of good will: the one preach Christ of contention, not sincerely, supposing to add affliction to my bonds: but the other of love, knowing that I am set for the defence of the gospel. What then? notwithstanding, every way, whether in pretence, or in truth, Christ is preached; and I therein do rejoice, yea, and will rejoice. For I know that this shall turn to my salvation through your prayer, and the supply of the Spirit of Jesus Christ, according to my earnest expectation and my hope, that in nothing I shall be ashamed, but that with all boldness, as always, so now also Christ shall be magnified in my body, whether it be by life, or by death. (vv. 12–20)

It is always a sad sign, and an evidence of spiritual decline, when the heart loses its interest in the message of grace. There are some so occupied with the deeper truths of the Word of God that they allow themselves to speak slightingly of the simplicity of the gospel. Paul was the preeminent teacher of the church, but to his last hour, his heart was filled with gospel zeal, and his sympathies were with the evangelist carrying the Word of Life to men dead in trespasses and in sins. Even in his prison house he rejoiced that his affairs had really tended to the progress of the gospel.

Satan, doubtless, hoped to hinder that work by locking up the apostle in a jail, but even there it became manifest to all Caesar's court, and to all others, that his bonds were for Christ's sake. The very soldiers appointed to guard him were brought thus to hear the glorious proclamation of grace to a guilty world. It is evident, both from verse 13 and verse 22 of chapter 4, that numbers of them believed. Who can fathom the joy that must have filled the heart of Paul as he led one guard after another to the Savior's feet! Just as when cast into the Philippian dungeon, he and his companion Silas were used to the conversion of the jailer and his household, so here, grace triumphed over all seemingly untoward circumstances, and the prison cell became a gospel chapel where souls were being born of God and stern Roman soldiers became themselves the captive servants of One greater than Caesar.

In verse 14 the apostle speaks of another cause of joy. While he was going about from place to place preaching the Word, there were gifted men who held back, feeling, perhaps, that they were in no sense on a par with him, and so they permitted the timidity and backwardness of the flesh to hinder their launching out in a work to which the Lord was beckoning them. But since he was in durance and could no longer go about from place to place in this happy service, numbers of these men came forward, and, for the Name's sake, went forth preaching the Word boldly without fear. On the other hand there were some restless men who had not commended themselves as fitted for evangelistic work, and while he was free, were kept in a place of subjection. But now that he was incarcerated they saw their opportunity to come to the front and went forth preaching Christ indeed with their lips, though their hearts were filled with envy and strife. But no jealous or envious thoughts entered the mind of Paul. He rejoiced in those who preached the Word through good will, out of love, knowing that he was appointed for the vindication of the gospel. Though he could not rejoice in the spirit that moved the others, he at least was gladdened to know that it was Christ who was being preached. And so he was thankful for every voice telling out the story of the cross. Nor would he permit anything to rob him of this joy.

How marked is the contrast between the spirit here exhibited and that which often prevails today. How seldom, in fact, do we see this simple unalloyed rejoicing that Christ is preached, let the aims and methods of the preacher be what they will. Untold harm is often done by harsh, captious criticism of young and earnest men, who often have much to learn and offend by their uncouthness, by their lack of discernment and understanding of the ways of the Lord, who nevertheless do preach Christ and win souls. And God has said, "He that winneth souls is wise"; or, as the Revised Version so strikingly puts it, "He that is wise winneth souls." Often have anxious souls been really hindered by the criticism of their elders in matters of this kind. Oh, for more of the spirit of Paul that would lead us to rejoice unfeignedly whenever Christ is preached, even though there be much to exercise our hearts and lead to prayer—and it may be to godly admonition at times, so far as methods and expressions are concerned, which if rightly dealt with now, may soon disappear as excrescences, when the earnest evangelist grows in grace and in the knowledge of the truth.

Verses 19–20 show us how the apostle relied upon the prayers of the people of God, and how encouraged he was by this abounding gospel testimony. He felt that it presaged his own deliverance, and pointed to the time when he would again be free according to his earnest expectation, and hope, to preach Christ openly and widely if it should be the will of God, or else to glorify Him in a martyr's death. He had but one ambition, and that, that Christ Himself should be magnified in his body whether by life or by death. No matter what he himself might be called upon to toil or suffer, if the One whom he had met on that never-to-be-forgotten day on the Damascus turnpike were exalted and honored—this would satisfy him.

It is this utter absence of self-seeking that commends any true servant of Christ. We see it strikingly in John the Baptist, who said, "He must increase, but I must decrease." It should be the one supreme characteristic of the evangelist, pastor, or teacher. And where this spirit of self-abnegation, for the glory of the Lord, is really found, it must commend the ministry, though it makes nothing of the minister. Oh, that one might enter more fully into it!

CHAPTER 4

CHRIST IS ALL IN LIFE OR DEATH

Philippians 1:21–26

For to me to live is Christ, and to die is gain. But if I live in the flesh, this is the fruit of my labour: yet what I shall choose I wot not. For I am in a strait betwixt two, having a desire to depart, and to be with Christ; which is far better: nevertheless to abide in the flesh is more needful for you. And having this confidence, I know that I shall abide and continue with you all for your furtherance and joy of faith; that your rejoicing may be more abundant in Jesus Christ for me by my coming to you again. (vv. 21–26)

To me to live is Christ" is Christian life and experience in its fullness. It has often been remarked, and is well worth remembering, that Christians have many experiences which are not properly Christian experience. The man described in Romans 7 is undergoing an experience which will be for his future blessing, but it is not proper Christian experience, though it is clearly enough the experience of a Christian. Christ Himself, so dominating and controlling the believer that his one object is to live to His glory, is what Paul has before him here. This should be the experience of Christians at all times. But, alas, how few of us enter into it in its entirety. It implies a surrendered will, and the body yielded to the Lord who has redeemed it, that it may be used only to His praise. This is life in its truest sense, and, probably, no one ever entered into it so fully as the apostle Paul.

We may, perhaps, better understand the experience, "To me to live is Christ," if we consider for a moment what life means to many others. The Christless businessman, whose one aim and object is to obtain wealth, might well say, "To me to live is money." The careless seeker after the world's pleasures, if he told the truth, would say, "To me to live is worldly pleasure." The carnal voluptuary given up to self-gratification, would say, "To me to live is self." The statesman, exulting in the plaudits of the people and craving world notoriety, might truthfully declare, "To me to live is fame and power." But Paul could say, and every Christian should be able to say, "To me to live is Christ."

And it is only such who can heartily add, "And to die is gain." Death is no enemy to the one to whom Christ is all. To live gives opportunity to manifest Christ down here; to die is to be with Christ, than which nothing could be more precious.

The apostle himself was in a dilemma as to which of these he would prefer, were the choice left to him. If permitted to continue in the body, he would have further opportunity of service for Him who had claimed him as His own and called him to this ministry. But, on the other hand, he longed "to depart and to be with Christ, which is far better." His had been a life of toil and suffering for Christ's sake, such as only a Spirit-sustained man could have endured without fainting. As he lay in the Roman prison, his heart longed for release—a release that would mean to be forever with Christ. Labor for Christ was sweet, but rest with Christ would be sweeter. Whitefield used to say, "I am often weary *in* the work, but never weary *of* it," and such was, doubtless, the attitude of our apostle. He loved to serve, yet longed too for the hour of release, with no selfish motive in it, for his one object was Christ, whether in life or in death.

It is amazing how anyone, with words such as these before him, could question for a moment that the Word of God teaches the consciousness of the spirit after death. Paul had no thought that his spirit would be buried in the grave with his body, or that his soul would sleep until the resurrection day. Death to him would be a departure, an exodus, a moving out of the travel-worn earthly tabernacle, and a going to be with Christ, until the first resurrection at the coming of the Lord.

As he weighs everything, the unselfishness of the man comes out strikingly. He sees the need of the church of God. As it is now, so it was then. There were many evangelists, or gospelers, but few teachers and pastors who really carried the people of God upon their hearts. He felt that to abide in the flesh was more needful for the flock than rest was for himself. So he says he has confidence that he should abide a little longer, and continue in this scene of labor for the furtherance and joy of faith of the people of God.

It is clear, I think, that he fully expected the Lord would permit him to revisit Philippi, that the rejoicings of the saints there might be more abundant in Christ Jesus on his behalf, through his coming to them again. They were his children in the faith: as a tender father he yearned over them, and longed to see them once more before closing his earthly ministry. We have no record in the Word of God as to whether this desire was fulfilled, but there are early church traditions which indicate that it was. At any rate, we know he was released from his first imprisonment and allowed to go about in freedom for several years before being again apprehended and martyred for the sake of Christ Jesus, his and our Lord, following Him thus even unto death.

CHAPTER 5

UNITY IN GOSPEL TESTIMONY

Philippians 1:27–30

Only let your conversation [or, behavior] be as it becometh the gospel of Christ: that whether I come and see you, or else be absent, I may hear of your affairs, that ye stand fast in one spirit, with one mind striving together for the faith of the gospel; and in nothing terrified by your adversaries: which is to them an evident token of perdition, but to you of salvation, and that of God. For unto you it is given in the behalf of Christ, not only to believe on him, but also to suffer for his sake; having the same conflict which ye saw in me, and now hear to be in me. (vv. 27–30)

The word *conversation*, as ordinarily employed by our forefathers, was of far wider scope than as generally used by us today. It meant not only the talk of the lips, though it included that, but it took in the entire behavior. The apostle's exhortation is to the effect that the whole manner of life of the people of God should be in accordance with the gospel of Christ. No more important message was ever committed to man than the word of reconciliation, which God has graciously entrusted to His people in this present dispensation of His mercy to a lost world. That gospel tells of the divine means of deliverance from the guilt and power of sin. How incongruous, then, if the testimonies of those who undertake to proclaim it with their mouths deny its power in their lives! A walk worthy of the gospel is a walk in the energy of the Holy Spirit. It is a life surrendered to Him, whose Lordship that gospel declares.

But it is not merely our individual responsibility to walk worthy of the gospel that the apostle here presses. He has rather before him assembly responsibility. He desires to hear of the affairs of the Philippians, that, as an assembly, they stand fast in one spirit with one mind, cooperating vigorously for the faith of the gospel. Nothing so mars gospel testimony as contention and self-seeking among God's people. Where jealousies and envyings come in to hinder the fellowship of those who should be standing together heart to heart and shoulder to shoulder for the truth of God, the effect on the world outside is most lamentable. This is particularly so with the unsaved members of believers' families. Nothing is more harmful to them than to find out that their elders are not commending the message they profess to love by unitedly standing together for the Word of God.

Is there not something here that deserves the careful consideration of many believers in the assemblies gathered to the name of the Lord Jesus Christ at the present time? Have we not allowed personalities, bickerings, and strife to greatly mar and hinder gospel testimony? On the other hand, it must be confessed that some, possessing evangelistic gift, have ignored, to a very marked degree, the importance of assembly fellowship in gospel testimony, launching forth often without the prayerful endorsement of older, more godly saints. They are afterward surprised and grieved that they do not find heartier cooperation on the part of assemblies whose judgment they ignored to begin with. The evangelist is the Lord's servant, and, therefore, is not subject to human dictation, but, on the other hand, fellowship involves mutual responsibility, and evangelists need to remember that gift is not necessarily piety nor does it always carry with it good judgment and sound wisdom. Therefore the importance of cultivating humility on the part of the servant, if he would have the hearty fellowship of assemblies in his work.

When there is this lowly, subject spirit manifested by the evangelist, and vigorous cooperation on the part of the assembly, God can be depended on to work in mighty power to the salvation of lost souls, and the blessing of His people; and this, to the enemy, is a condition he most dreads. Where an assembly is walking in love and exercised about the Lord's things in this scene, they need not fear the attacks of evil powers, natural or supernatural, from without. These unholy hosts read their own doom in the happy fellowship of the saints of God and see in it a proof of the truth of the Lord's words, "Upon this rock I will build [mine assembly]; and the gates of hell shall not prevail against it." The thought that many have in mind in reading this Scripture seems to be that the assembly of God is as a city besieged, beleaguered by the enemies of the Lord and carrying on a defensive warfare, though with the pledge of eventual victory. This, however, is far from fulfilling the picture presented by our Lord. An invading or besieging army does not carry the gates of its cities with it. It is hell, or hades, the realm of darkness, that is being besieged by the forces of light who are carrying on, not a defensive, but an offensive warfare, and to them the promise is given that "the gates of hell shall not prevail." This is the "perdition" spoken of in verse 28.

Such fellowship as that which the apostle brings before us, cannot be fully entered into apart from suffering, but this is to be esteemed as a privilege by those who fight under the banner of the risen Lord. It is given to such, as it were a guerdon greatly to be desired, in behalf of Christ Himself, not only to trust in Him as Savior, but manfully to toil and suffer, that His name may be glorified in the scene where He Himself was rejected and crucified, and over which He is soon coming to reign.

How blessedly and how fully had the apostle entered into this! With what joy did he endure and suffer that Christ might be glorified! Yea, at the very time of writing this letter he was the prisoner of the Lord in a Roman prison, while saints at Philippi, some of them at least, were living in comfort and slothfulness, and some even stooping to quarreling among themselves. The apostle's words in verse 30 would prove, surely, a home-thrust to such as these, stirring heart and conscience, as they contrasted their easygoing lives with the sufferings of Christ's dear servant, who was in prison because of his unselfish devotion to the Lord he loved. May we learn to walk in the same spirit, and mind the same things!

PART 2

CHRIST, THE BELIEVER'S EXAMPLE, AND THE LOWLY MIND

CHAPTER 6

"OTHERS"

Philippians 2:1–4

If there be therefore any consolation in Christ, if any comfort of love, if any fellowship of the Spirit, if any bowels and mercies, fulfil ye my joy, that ye be likeminded, having the same love, being of one accord, of one mind. Let nothing be done through strife or vainglory; but in lowliness of mind let each esteem other better than themselves. Look not every man on his own things, but every man also on the things of others. (vv. 1–4)

The last word of this section is the keynote—*others*. This was the overpowering, dominating note in the life of our Lord on earth and because of this He died. "[He] came not to be ministered unto, but to minister, and to give his life a ransom for"—others! He lived for others; He died for others. Selfishness He knew not. Unselfish devotion for the good of others summed up His whole life, and all in subjection to the Father's will. For God, the Father Himself, lives, reverently be it said, for others. He finds His delight, His joy, in lavishing blessing on others. He pours His rain, and sends His sunshine upon the just and the unjust alike. He gave His Son for others. Having not withheld His own Son, but delivered Him up for us all, how will He not with Him also freely give us all things?—we, who are included in the others for whom the Lord Jesus Christ endured so much. What wonder then that, if we would follow His steps, we find ourselves called upon to live for others, and even to lay down our lives for the brethren!

In the first verse, the *if* does not imply that there might not be consolation in Christ, comfort of love, and fellowship of the Spirit, coupled with tender mercies toward all for whom Christ died. It rather has the force of since—it is an intensive form of saying, Since you know there are consolations and comforts in Christ. If these things are blessed realities, how incongruous for a believer to act as though they were nonexistent! Drinking in the spirit of Christ, we exemplify the mind of Christ. And so the apostle exhorts the saints to fulfill his cup of joy by like-mindedness among themselves, with equal love toward one another, being of one accord, of one mind.

It is very evident that Christians will never see eye to eye on all points. We are so largely influenced by habits, by environment, by education, by the measure of intellectual and spiritual apprehension to which we have attained, that it is an impossibility to find any number of people who look at everything from the same standpoint. How then can such be of one mind? The apostle himself explains it elsewhere when he says, "I think also that I have the mind of Christ." The "mind of Christ" is the lowly mind. And, if we are all of this mind, we shall walk together in love, considering one another, and seeking rather to be helpers of one another's faith, than challenging each other's convictions.

This is emphasized in the third verse, "Let nothing be done through strife or vainglory." It is possible, as verses 15–16 of chapter 1 have already shown us, to be controlled by this spirit of strife and vainglory, even in connection with the holy things of the Lord. But Paul himself has furnished us a beautiful example of that lowliness of mind of which he speaks, when he could rejoice even though Christ were preached in contention.

Nothing is less suited to a follower of the meek and lowly Son of Man than a contentious spirit and vainglorious bearing. Boasting and bitter words ill become one who has taken the place of death with Christ. If, in lowliness of mind, each esteems others better than himself, how impossible for strife and contention to come in. Alas, that it is so much easier to speak or write of these things than to practically demonstrate them!

It is not in the natural man to live out what is here inculcated. The man after the flesh "looks out for number one," as he puts it, and is fond of reminding himself, and his fellows, that "charity begins at home." But the Christian is exhorted to look, not on his own things, but on the things of others. A heavenly principle this, surely, and only to be attained by a heavenly man, one who walks in fellowship with Him who came from heaven to manifest His love for others. It is characteristic of man's deceitful natural heart to suppose that his greatest pleasure can be found in ministering to his own desires. But the truest happiness is the result of unselfish devotion to the things of others. Were this ever kept in mind, what unhappy experiences would many of God's dear children be spared, and how glad and joyous would fellowship in Christ become.

CHAPTER 7

"THE KENOSIS"

Philippians 2:5–8

Let this mind be in you, which was also in Christ Jesus: who, being in the form of God, thought it not robbery to be equal with God: but made himself of no reputation, and took upon him the form of a servant, and was made in the likeness of men: and being found in fashion as a man, he humbled himself, and became obedient unto death, even the death of the cross. (vv. 5–8)

We now come to consider one of the most sublime and wonderful mysteries in all Scripture: what has been called by theologians, "The Doctrine of the Kenosis." The title comes from the Greek expression rendered in our King James Version, "made Himself of no reputation"—an expression which really means "emptied Himself" or "divested Himself." Its full force will come before us as we proceed with our study.

It is a noticeable thing that doctrines are never presented in Scripture merely as dogmas to be accepted by the faithful on pain of expulsion from the Christian company. The most important doctrines are brought in by the Holy Spirit in what we might call an exceedingly natural way. I do not use the word *natural* here in contrast to *spiritual*, but rather in the sense simply of sequence to the subject, introduced without special emphasis. In this particular instance before us, the doctrine of our Lord's self-emptying comes in simply as the supreme illustration of that lowliness of mind which should characterize all who profess to be followers of the Savior. It follows naturally upon the exhortation of the fourth verse, which we have already considered.

"Let this mind be in you, which was also in Christ Jesus" is the way the subject is introduced. This mind is the lowly mind, as it is written, "Even Christ pleased not himself." And the exemplification of this is at once abruptly introduced. He existed from all eternity in the form of God. It is a declaration of His true Deity. No creature could exist in the form of God. Lucifer aspired to this, and for his impiety was hurled down from the archangel's throne. Our Lord Jesus Christ was in the full enjoyment of this by right, because He was the eternal Son. He thought equality with God not a thing to be grasped or held on to. Equal with God He was, but He chose to take the place of subjection and lowliness. He chose to step down from that sublime height that belonged to Him, even "the glory which [He] had with [the Father] before the world was," and took the servant's form to do the Father's will.

The first man aspired to be as God and fell. The second man, the Lord from heaven, came, as we sometimes sing,

> From Godhead's fullest glory,
> Down to Calvary's depth of woe.

He would not retain the outward semblance of Deity. He relinquished His rightful position to become the Savior of sinners. In order to do this He emptied Himself, or divested Himself, of His divine prerogatives.

Let there be no mistake as to this. While we reverently put off our shoes from our feet, and draw near to behold this great sight, let us not fear to accept the declaration of Holy Scripture in all its fullness. He divested Himself of something—but of what? Not of His Deity, for that could not be. He was ever the Son of the Father, and, as such, a divine person. He could take manhood into union with Deity, but He could not cease to be Divine. Of what, then, did He divest Himself? Surely of His rights as God the Son. He chose to come to earth to take a place of subjection. He took upon Him the form of a servant and was made in the likeness of men.

Observe the distinction brought out in these two verses. He existed from all eternity in the form of God. He came here to take the form of a servant. Angels are servants, but "He took not hold of angels," we are told in the epistle to the Hebrews (2:16 DARBY). He became in the likeness of men. It was all voluntary on His part. And, as a man on earth, He chose to be guided by the Holy Spirit. He daily received from the Father, through the Word of God, the instruction which it became Him, as a Man, to receive. His mighty works of power were not wrought by His own divine omnipotence alone. He chose that they should be wrought in the power of the Holy Spirit. This is the precious and important doctrine of the Kenosis as revealed in Scripture in contrast with the false teaching of men.

Men have added to this what Scripture does not say. They have declared that when He came to earth He ceased to be God, that He became but an ignorant Galilean peasant. Hence His knowledge of divine mysteries was no greater than what might have been expected of any other good man of His day and generation. Therefore His testimony as to the inspiration of Scripture has no real weight. He did not know more than others of His day knew. He was not competent to speak as to the authors of the Old Testament books. He thought Daniel wrote the book that bears his name and that Moses penned the Pentateuch. But the wiseacres of today do not hesitate to declare that He was wrong, and they base their declaration on the position above taken. He emptied Himself of His divine knowledge they say, therefore He could not speak with authority.

CHAPTER 8

THE EXALTATION OF THE MAN CHRIST JESUS

Philippians 2:9–11

Wherefore God also hath highly exalted him, and given him a name which is above every name: that at the name of Jesus every knee should bow, of things in heaven, and things in earth, and things under the earth [or, of heavenly, earthly, and infernal beings]; and that every tongue should confess that Jesus Christ is Lord, to the glory of God the Father. (vv. 9–11)

This is the glorious fulfillment of the prophecy of Psalm 110—a prophecy used by our Lord to confound the cavilers of His day, who professed to be waiting for the promised Messiah, but rejected His deity. "[Jehovah] said unto my Lord, Sit thou at my right hand, until I make thine enemies thy footstool" (v. 1). He is David's Son—the Branch of David, yet David calls Him Lord, because He is likewise the Root of David. He descended from Jesse's son, yet the son of Jesse came into being through Him. His exaltation as man to the throne of God is not only Jehovah's attestation of perfect satisfaction in His work, but also the recognition of His equality with Himself. This Man, who had so humbled Himself as to go even to the death of the cross, is Jehovah's Fellow, as Zechariah 13:7 declares. Of none but a divine Person could such language be rightly used.

It is interesting to notice that God never permitted one indignity to be put upon the body of His Son after His work was finished, as the Roman soldier, having pierced His side, released the atoning blood. No enemies' hands thenceforth touched it. Loving disciples tenderly took it down from the cross and reverently laid it away in Joseph's new tomb after wrapping it in the linen clothes.

Then, upon the expiration of the time appointed, He who had died came forth in resurrection life, and God the Father received Him up into glory. He has highly exalted Him and given Him a name that is above every name. He is the preeminent one in every sphere. How suited it is that His glory should thus answer to His shame. "*As* many were astonished at Him . . . *so* shall He astonish many nations" (Isa. 52:14–15, literal rendering). God has ordained it, and so it must be. At the name of Jesus—His personal name, which means Jehovah-the-Savior—the name borne upon the title placed above His head as He hung upon the cross—every knee shall bow: heavenly, earthly, and infernal beings—all must own Him Lord of all.

Observe that here, where it is a question of the recognition of His authority, three spheres are brought in, comprising all created intelligent beings—in heaven, earth, and hell. There will be no exceptions. All must confess His Lordship to the glory of God the Father. All must bow in lowly submissiveness at the mention of the name of the Crucified.

Does this then imply universal salvation, even the final restoration of Satan and his hosts, as some have taught? Surely not.

Subjugation is one thing; reconciliation is another. When the latter is in question, we have but two spheres mentioned, as in Colossians 1:20: "Having made peace by the blood of his cross, by him to reconcile all things unto himself; by him, I say, whether they be things in earth, or things in heaven." There is here no mention of the underworld. The lost will never be reconciled. Heaven and earth will eventually be filled with happy beings who have been redeemed to God by the precious blood of Christ. Then reconciliation will be complete.

But "under the earth" will be those who "have their part" in the outer darkness, the lake of fire. They flaunted Christ's authority on earth. They will have to own it in hell! They refused to heed the call of grace and be reconciled to God in the day when they might have been saved. In the pit of woe no gospel message will ever be proclaimed, but the authority of the Lord Jesus Christ will be supremely enforced there too. There will be no disorder in hell; no further rebellion will be permitted. All must bow at the name of Jesus and every tongue confess Him Lord. Scripture depicts no wild pandemonium when describing the abode of the lost.

How blessed to own His Lordship now, according as it is written, "That if thou shalt confess with thy mouth [Jesus as Lord], and shalt believe in thine heart that God hath raised him from the dead, thou shalt be saved. For with the heart man believeth unto righteousness; and with the mouth confession is made unto salvation" (Rom. 10:9–10). How fitting it is that such, and such alone, should be eternally saved as a result of the work of the cross.

CHAPTER 9

"WORKING OUT SALVATION"

Philippians 2:12–16

Wherefore, my beloved, as ye have always obeyed, not as in my presence only, but now much more in my absence, work out your own salvation with fear and trembling. For it is God which worketh in you both to will and to do of his good pleasure. Do all things without murmurings and disputings: that ye may be blameless and harmless, the sons of God, without rebuke, in the midst of a crooked and perverse nation, among whom ye shine as lights in the world; holding forth the word of life; that I may rejoice in the day of Christ, that I have not run in vain, neither laboured in vain. (vv. 12–16)

Having thus occupied the hearts of the saints at Philippi with the self-abnegation of our Lord Jesus Christ, the apostle, as guided by the Holy Spirit, goes on, in the balance of this chapter, to apply the truth in a practical way.

First, the verses now before us refer to assembly life and responsibility. Then, from verse 17 to the end of this chapter, three men are brought before us who were seeking to manifest in their lives the devotedness and self-denying concern for others that was seen in Christ as a man on earth.

46

Verse 12 has often perplexed those who thought they saw clearly from Scripture the simplicity of salvation by grace, apart from works. Here, in seeming contrast to this, the apostle tells the saints to work out their own salvation, and that with fear and trembling, as though possibly there were danger that salvation might be forfeited because of failure in properly working it out.

Notice first, however, that the apostle does not speak of working for salvation, but of working it out, which is a very different thing. One might instance the quaint saying of the little girl who listened to a legal sermon preached upon this text by a minister who was insisting that none could be saved by grace alone, but all must work out their own salvation. Innocently she asked at the close of the service, "Mother, how can you work it out if you haven't got it in?" If it were individual salvation that is here contemplated, it might be enough to say—it is your own, therefore, manifest it—work it out. But there is really more than this. For, taken in its full connection, it will be seen the passage refers to assembly salvation, rather than to the individual: that is, direction is given to an assembly of Christians (exposed to difficulties from without and from within, passing through a world where all is in opposition to the testimony committed to them), showing them how to go on in fellowship together in spite of the fact that each individual has within him a corrupt nature, which will manifest itself to the detriment of the whole assembly, if given occasion.

We have already noticed that there was some difficulty in the Philippian assembly between two sisters of prominence, Euodia and Syntyche. This might easily become the occasion for distressing quarrels, and even division, if not judged in the presence of the Lord. Similar things might arise from time to time, and would need to be carefully watched against. When the apostle himself was with them, they could refer all such matters to him, and he would, so to speak, work out their salvation from these perplexities. He would advise and guide as needed. Now he is far away, a prisoner for the gospel's sake, and cannot personally give the help he might desire. He, therefore, directs them in his absence, as obedient children, to work out their own salvation in godly fear, and with exercise of soul, lest they depart from the right path, or miss the mind of God.

Viewed from this standpoint, how salutary are his words for all future generations of Christians! There is no assembly of saints on earth but will probably, sooner or later, have its internal differences, and the advice or command here given applies in just such cases. It is God's way that assemblies should be put right from within by self-judgment in His presence and submission to His word.

How often do saints take the very opposite method. Questions arise to trouble and perplex, differences of judgment occur, and bickerings and quarrels begin.

Instead of coming together in the presence of God for humiliation and guidance, seeking His mind from His own Word and acting accordingly, they apply to this one or that one outside for help—often only to have things worse complicated. Those engaged in the ministry of the Word, traveling from place to place, are perhaps appealed to and requested to adjudicate in matters that often only disturb their spirits, and, after all, cannot really effect the salvation of the assembly from the troubles that have arisen.

It is easy to see how the clerical system arose from such experiences. We see in the early church, men of the stamp of Diotrephes, who loved to have the pre-eminence, and Nicolaitanes, that is, rulers of the people, who sought to bring the saints into bondage. And, on the other hand, it was very early made manifest that believers generally found it much easier to apply to noted preachers or teachers for help than to be cast directly upon God and His Word themselves. Thus gifted men became a court of appeal, and, eventually, were recognized as "the clergy." The same principle easily creeps in wherever saints look to men rather than to God and His Word. If it be said that they are too ignorant to know how to settle their differences, yet let it be remembered they have God, and the word of His grace. If there be but humility and waiting upon Him, refusing to move until they find direction in the Book, He can be depended upon to help them work out their own salvation from whatever perplexing circumstances have arisen. He does not cast them upon their own resources but on His Word, on Himself, who works in them the will to do His good pleasure. This does not mean that they should ignore or despise the advice and sound judgment of others—but they are not dependent upon it.

In verses 14–16 we see this working out of assembly salvation practically demonstrated. Murmurings and disputings must be judged in the presence of God. Instead of backbiting and gossiping about matters, let the saints come together before the Lord and deal with them in the light of His revealed Word. Thus they shall be blameless and harmless, the sons of God indeed, without rebuke walking in a manner worthy of the Lord, in the midst of a crooked and perverse generation among whom they shine as lights in this dark world. Thus judging what would hinder fellowship within, they are in a suited condition to be a testimony to the power of grace to those without. And, as the apostle has already emphasized for us in chapter 1, nothing so delivers believers from self-occupation as occupation with Christ and the presentation of Christ to those still in their sins. They who are busy holding forth the Word of Life have no time for selfish quarreling among themselves.

In so walking, the saints would give joy to the heart of the apostle, and he could rejoice in the day of Christ: that is, it would be manifest at His judgment seat that his labors in Philippi had not been in vain. The godly order and devoted gospel testimony would together witness to the reality of the work of God in and among them.

Thus we see that "working out our own salvation" is simply submitting to the truth of God after we have been saved, in order that we may glorify Him, whether as individuals or assemblies of saints in the place of testimony. This will be "with fear and trembling" as we realize our liability to err, the faultiness of our understanding, and the holiness of the One whom we are called to serve in this scene.

CHAPTER 10

THE MIND OF CHRIST EXEMPLIFIED IN THE APOSTLE PAUL

Philippians 2:17–18

Yea, and if I be offered upon the sacrifice and service of your faith, I joy, and rejoice with you all. For the same cause also do ye joy, and rejoice with me. (vv. 17–18)

The apostolic writer now goes on to cite, though in an apparently casual way, three examples of men of like passions with their fellow believers who have exemplified in their ways the spirit of Christ. The first of these is himself and of his testimony we shall now speak. The other two are Timothy and Epaphroditus, whose lowly ways and devoted service will occupy us later.

Possibly no other mortal man ever drank into the spirit of Christ so deeply as the great apostle to the Gentiles. Once a proud, haughty Pharisee, glorying in his own righteousness, burning with indignant bigotry against any who pretended to a higher revelation than that given in Judaism, he had been transformed by a sight of the glorified Christ, when, religious persecutor as he was, he was hurrying to Damascus to apprehend any who confessed the name of Jesus. The sight of the once-crucified, but now enthroned Savior, at God's right hand, was the means of a conversion so radical and so sudden, that probably no other since has been so intense.

From that moment it was the one desire of his soul, overmastering all else, the inmost yearning of his being, to manifest Christ in all his ways. Yet he was not an absolutely sinless man, nor without the infirmities common to the human race. But he was one who ever sought to judge himself in the light of the cross of Christ, with the power of Christ resting upon him. His whole philosophy of life is summed up in his fervent words to the Galatians, "But God forbid that I should glory, save in the cross of our Lord Jesus Christ, by whom the world is crucified unto me, and I unto the world" (Gal. 6:14).

It was in this spirit that he could write to his beloved Philippians, "Yea, and if I be offered [literally "poured out"] upon the sacrifice and service of your faith, I joy, and rejoice with you all." He had just told them that his joy in the day of Christ would be to find them approved, as having walked before God in this scene as unrebuked saints earnestly engaged in holding forth the Word of Life in a dark world: their abundant service and the reward meted out to them, he would look upon as reward to himself. He would thus feel that he had not run in vain, neither labored in vain. He was willing to count all his service as but an adjunct of theirs, to have their labors and devotedness looked upon as the completion of a work of which his was just the beginning.

In order properly to understand this seventeenth verse, it is necessary to ob-serve carefully what the apostle has in mind. When he says, "If I be poured out upon the sacrifice of your faith," he alludes to the drink offering. This was a cup of wine, which was poured out upon the burnt offering, and was typical of the out-pouring of our Lord Jesus Christ's soul unto death, the voluntary surrender of everything that might naturally be expected to contribute to his joys as a man. Wine is the symbol of gladness. What man ever deserved to be happier than the Lord Jesus Christ? To whom was gladness a righteous due, if not to Him? Yet, in infinite grace, He became "a man of sorrows, and acquainted with grief."

The burnt offering spoke of Him in the highest sense as offering Himself without spot to God, but on our behalf. In the sacrificial service, the burnt of-fering having been slain was cut in its pieces, was washed with water, then laid in order upon the fire of the altar and wholly consumed. The drink offering was simply poured out upon it, and in a moment was lost to sight. Now, with this in mind, consider the beauty of the figure the apostle here employs. Whatever service the Philippians might be able to render to the Lord would be in fellow-ship with Christ, and thus their devotedness could be viewed as an offering or a sacrifice of a sweet-smelling savor unto God. It was the result of lives surrendered to the Lord, and Paul was willing that his labor should be simply looked upon as the adjunct of theirs, as the drink offering poured upon the burnt offering.

What sublime self-abnegation was this! What delight in the labors of others! What absence of that which sometimes is so abhorrent in professed Christian service today! Laborers sometimes are jealous of the ministry of others, and envious of a success in which they think they have not shared. There was no such spirit in the apostle Paul. He rejoiced in everything that the Lord did through others, and his jealousy was only for the glory of God.

And so in this he followed Christ, and he could confidently appeal to them to follow him, as he walked in His steps. So he would have them joy and rejoice with him in the mutual devotedness of both.

It is significant that he speaks of himself and his service in this incidental way—in but one verse. When he turns to write of his fellow laborer, Timothy, and of their messenger, Epaphroditus, how much more he has to say. He could dwell with delight on the labors and service of others, but when writing of himself, as he tells us elsewhere, he felt as though he were speaking as a fool.

CHAPTER 11

TIMOTHY, THE UNSELFISH PASTOR

Philippians 2:19–24

But I trust in the Lord Jesus to send Timotheus shortly unto you, that I also may be of good comfort, when I know your state. For I have no man likeminded, who will naturally care for your state. For all seek their own, not the things which are Jesus Christ's. But ye know the proof of him, that, as a son with the father, he hath served with me in the gospel. Him therefore I hope to send presently, so soon as I shall see how it will go with me. But I trust in the Lord that I also myself shall come shortly. (vv. 19–24)

Paul was not only an ardent evangelist, but he was also the prince of teachers, and, like his fellow apostle Peter, a true pastor, or shepherd, of the flock of Christ. In this latter respect the young preacher Timothy was his ardent imitator. Whatever other gifts he may have had, that special gift that was given him in connection with the laying on of the elder brethren's hands, when he went out in the work of the Lord, was probably that of the pastor. This is perhaps one of the rarest, and yet one of the most needed, of all the gifts given by an ascended Christ for the edification of His church. The evangelist ministers to those without

Christ; the teacher instructs those already saved; the pastor is more concerned about the state of soul of the believer than as to his knowledge of abstract truth, though recognizing, of course, that saints are formed by the truth, and that a right state of soul and a walk in the truth go together.

Paul, therefore, was anxious to send Timothy to Philippi, that he might be a help and a means of blessing to the assembly there, trusting that he might be used of God to weld their hearts into one, and deliver them from the dissensions that had come in through the misunderstanding between Euodia and Syntyche. He felt that he could depend on Timothy's judgment, and he counted on being himself comforted when he actually knew their state.

As often pointed out by others, and clearly developed in different parts of Scripture, our standing before God is one thing, our actual state is another. It was as to the latter that Paul was concerned. He did not know of anyone else with the same unselfish shepherd heart as Timothy, who would whole-souledly care for their state. The word *naturally* does not adequately give the thought. Timothy's pastoral concern was not a gift of nature, but a spiritual one, the result of exercise of soul before God. His whole soul was stirred with concern for the Lord's people. Of others, however gifted in various ways, the apostle could only sadly say, "They seek their own, and not the things which are Jesus Christ's."

It is quite possible to be an admired teacher, upon whose words thousands hang, or an eloquent evangelist with eager multitudes flocking to listen with delight to his messages, and yet be a vain self-seeker, using the very gift that God has given, for personal aggrandizement, or to obtain wealth, even while professing to care little or nothing for money. But the more marked the pastoral gift, of very necessity the more unselfishly devoted must the servant be. It will be his great ambition to feed the flock and shield them from their dangers.

The patriarch Jacob is an apt illustration of the true shepherd. Despite all his failures, and the fact that he was largely under the discipline of God through the greater part of his life, he was, nevertheless, a lover of the flock and ever considerate of their interests. Speaking to Laban, his father-in-law, he could honestly say as he looked back over his years of caring for the sheep, "Thus I was; in the day the drought consumed me, and the frost by night; and my sleep departed from mine eyes" (Gen. 31:40). And in expostulating with his brother Esau, who would have him hurry on with all his host, he says, "My lord knoweth that the children are tender, and the flocks and herds with young are with me: and if men should overdrive them one day, all the flock will die" (Gen. 33:13). A Diotrephes might try to cajole or coerce the flock into submission to his own imperious will, but a God-appointed shepherd will seek to lead on safely, wearing himself out for the blessing of others—not seeking to impress his own will, but to serve the Lord, and to exalt Him.

As a son with a father, Timothy had commended himself to the aged apostle, serving with him in the gospel in all lowliness and humility. Youth is often exceedingly energetic, and impatient of restraint. Age is inclined, perhaps, to be overcautious and slow in coming to conclusions, and it often is a great difficulty for two, so wide apart in years as Paul and Timothy, to labor together happily. But where the younger man manifests the spirit that was in Timothy, and the elder seeks only the glory of God and the blessing of His people, such fellowship in service becomes indeed blessed.

Having thus proven himself, Paul could trust Timothy on a mission such as that upon which he was about to send him. He was waiting to learn the outcome of his appeal to Caesar, and then he hoped to send him on to Philippi to be a healer of dissensions, and thus a means of cheer and consolation to the assembly. Timothy followed Paul as he followed Christ. He thus became the second in this company of men who were worthy to be held up as examples of those who manifested the mind of Christ.

It was the apostle's desire and hope to follow later himself and again visit his beloved Philippians. But whether this yearning was ever fulfilled we perhaps shall never know, until all is manifested at the judgment seat of Christ. Precious is the faith that can leave all with Him, assured that His ways are always perfect—always best!

CHAPTER 12

EPAPHRODITUS, THE DEVOTED MESSENGER

Philippians 2:25–30

Yet I supposed it necessary to send to you Epaphroditus, my brother, and companion in labour, and fellowsoldier, but your messenger, and he that ministered to my wants. For he longed after you all, and was full of heaviness, because that ye had heard that he had been sick. For indeed he was sick nigh unto death: but God had mercy on him; and not on him only, but on me also, lest I should have sorrow upon sorrow. I sent him therefore the more carefully, that, when ye see him again, ye may rejoice, and that I may be the less sorrowful. Receive him therefore in the Lord with all gladness; and hold such in reputation: because for the work of Christ he was nigh unto death, not regarding his life, to supply your lack of service toward me. (vv. 25–30)

It was Epaphroditus who had brought the bounty of the Philippian saints to Paul, their father in Christ. Burning with love toward the Lord's dear servant who was shut up in prison for the gospel's sake, he took the long journey from

Macedonia to Rome, the world's metropolis (whether by land or sea we have now no means of knowing), in order to assure him of the love and esteem of the assembly, and relieve his necessities by their gift.

Having accomplished his purpose, he fell sick, possibly overcome by the Roman fever, so dangerous to strangers unacclimated. That his illness was a protracted one is evident, for, before he became convalescent, time enough had elapsed for word of his condition to reach the Philippians, and for a return message to get back to him, expressing their solicitude for his health and anxiety that he be restored to them again. It is touching to notice that Epaphroditus himself did not seem to be nearly so much concerned about his own illness as he was that it had been the cause of sorrow to them. He was one of those thoroughly self-denying men whose motto might well be expressed in the one word upon which we have already dwelt, "Others."

Now that he was well again he was anxious to be on his way, in order that he might comfort the assembly by his presence among them again, and by bringing to them this Philippian epistle, though it must have been hard for him to leave the apostle still a prisoner. It is evident from verse 3 of chapter 4 that he acted as amanuensis in the writing of this letter, which precious parchment he carried to Philippi, and thus preserved it for us and for all saints to the end of time—yea, and we may say forever!

Of Epaphroditus we know nothing save what is here recorded, unless, as some think, he is to be identified with the Epaphras mentioned in the epistle to the Colossians. Epaphroditus means "favored of Aphrodite"—the Greek goddess of love and beauty, answering to the Roman Venus. This makes it manifest that he was of heathen parentage, but he had been brought to know Christ. Epaphras is said to be a diminutive of the same word with the name of the heathen goddess omitted and, therefore, simply meaning "graced" or "favored."

Having been won to Christ, he was characterized by a godly zeal to make Him known to others, and to build up and lead on those already saved. He was the exemplification of the mind of Christ as set forth in the beginning of this chapter. He may not have been physically strong, but, at any rate, he was a man who did not spare himself, and for the work of Christ he was sick nigh unto death. It is evident that sickness is not always the result of sin, as some have taught. In the case of this devoted man of God, it was the result of his self-denying activity on behalf of those to whom he ministered. His illness was the cause of deep sorrow to Paul himself, and, no doubt, led to much prayer on his behalf, and God answered, showing mercy, and raised him up.

Let it be noted that the apostle did not consider he had any right to demand physical healing even for so faithful a laborer as Epaphroditus. Paul recognized it as simply the mercy of God, not as that to which saints have a right. This is true divine healing. And let it be remembered that sickness may be as really from God as health. It is clear that Paul never held or taught "healing in the atonement" and, therefore, the birthright privilege of all Christians. Nor do we ever read of him or his fellow laborers being miraculously healed. Paul himself, Trophimus, Timothy, and Epaphroditus, all bear witness to the contrary. The apostle urges the saints to receive their messenger when he should return to them with all gladness, and commands them to hold such in reputation, because for the work of Christ he had been sick, nigh unto death, not regarding his life in order to serve Paul in their stead.

Such are the men whom God delights to honor. Like the Lord Jesus, Epaphroditus made himself of no reputation, and because of his very lowliness he is to be held in reputation. The man who holds himself as one worthy of honor and esteem is not the one whom God calls upon the saints thus to recognize. But he who is willing to take the lowly path, seeking not great things for himself, is the man whom the Lord will exalt in due time.

Salutary lessons are thus manifested in all these three devoted men of God upon whose self-denying ways we have meditated. May we have grace to follow them as they followed Christ!

PART 3

CHRIST, THE BELIEVER'S OBJECT, AND THE STEADFAST MIND

CHAPTER 13

"REJOICE"

Philippians 3:1–3

Finally, my brethren, rejoice in the Lord. To write the same things to you, to me indeed is not grievous, but for you it is safe. Beware of dogs, beware of evil workers, beware of the concision. For we are the circumcision, which worship God in the spirit, and rejoice in Christ Jesus, and have no confidence in the flesh. (vv. 1–3)

Careful students of the epistles of Paul cannot but notice a peculiarity that frequently occurs in them. Having concluded the main part of his treatise, he seems about to come to an abrupt conclusion then suddenly is moved by the Spirit of God to launch out into an altogether different line of things, which comes in as a kind of a parenthesis before he actually finishes his letter. An instance of this may be seen in the epistle to the Ephesians by comparing the first verses of chapters 3 and 4. It is plain that all of chapter 3, after verse 1, comes in parenthetically, and in chapter 4 he concludes what he started to say. Here in Philippians we have a similar case: "Finally, my brethren," he writes, "rejoice in the Lord." Yet, when we come to 4:8 where he introduces his closing remarks, we again have the same expression: "Finally, brethren." All of chapter 3 is a new subject, which, as we might think, he had no intention of discussing until pressed by the Holy Spirit to bring in a message for which we can truly thank God as we would have lost much precious ministry had it been omitted.

It has often been said that this letter is the epistle of joy, and indeed it is. The apostle himself writes with his own heart filled with the joyful recollection of his past experiences in connection with those scenes so dear to him. He desires them to fulfill his joy, to share with him in the gladness that was his in Christ, and so we have this brief exhortation, "Rejoice in the Lord." Circumstances may at times be anything but conducive to either peace or gladness, yet the trusting soul can always look above the fitful scenes of earth to the throne where Christ sits exalted as Lord at God's right hand. He is over all. There are no second causes with Him. "Shall there be evil in the city and the Lord hath not done it?" asks the prophet. It is "evil," not in the sense of sin, of course, but of calamity, even if that calamity be the result of sin. Nevertheless, it cannot come save as permitted by the Lord. And knowing that "all things work together for good to those who love God, who are the called according to his purpose," why should the believer either doubt or fear? Waves may roll high, stormy winds may beat tempestuously, all to which the heart had clung may seem to be swept away, but Christ abides unchanged and unchangeable, the everlasting portion of those who trust His grace.

We read on one occasion how David, when the people spoke of stoning him because of a calamitous event for which they held him largely responsible, "encouraged himself in the LORD his God." "The joy of the LORD is your strength," Nehemiah reminded the remnant of Israel. Before returning to the Father's house from which He came, the Lord Jesus imparted His joy to the trembling company of His disciples. Therefore, it is not only the Christian's privilege, but we may even say, his duty, to constantly rejoice in the Lord. Holiness and happiness are intimately linked together.

And yet how often we need to be reminded of this, as our apostle does here: "To write the same things to you, to me indeed is not [irksome], but for you it is safe." It is well that we should frequently be exhorted to "rejoice in the Lord."

But now the mind of the Spirit refers to another line of things entirely. For our busy enemy has so many agencies through which he seeks to rob us of that joy in the Lord that is our rightful portion, that three times over in the second verse we have the significant word *beware*.

"Beware of dogs." The Jew used this opprobrious title when speaking of the Gentiles, who did not bear in their bodies the mark of the Abrahamic covenant. But in the prophet Isaiah, God uses the term to distinguish false pastors or shepherds in Israel: "His watchmen are blind: they are all ignorant, they are all dumb dogs, they cannot bark; sleeping, lying down, loving to slumber. Yea, they are greedy dogs which can never have enough, and they are shepherds that cannot understand: they all look to their own way, every one for his gain, from his quarter" (56:10–11). And it is plain that when the apostle Peter says, "The dog has turned to his own vomit again," it symbolizes the false religious teacher going back to the things he once professed to abhor.

Now the Philippians, like the early Christians in general, were peculiarly exposed to the ravages of such "dogs." Evil teachers they were from Judaism among the flock of Christ with the purpose of perverting the saints and leading them back into bondage, and that for their own selfish ends. They are here, by the Holy Spirit, designated by this opprobrious term. They were introducing themselves among the assemblies of God to rend the flock of Christ, that they might have special recognition as leaders in the new company. Professing to be ministers of Christ, they were in reality servants of Satan as their works proved. No heart have they for the afflicted sheep and lambs for whom Christ died. They would feed themselves and not the flock, and their judgment is assured.

Consequently he adds, "Beware of evil workers." We need not necessarily distinguish the evil workers from the dogs, for false teachers, whatever their profession of righteousness, are, nevertheless, workers of iniquity. Another figure employed by the Lord in referring to the same general class is that of "wolves in sheep's clothing"—deceiving, misleading, destroying, working havoc among those who confess Christ's precious name. Legality, while professing to have in view greater righteousness than that produced by grace, yet proves to be, as the law itself is, simply "the strength of sin" (see 1 Cor. 15:56).

"Beware of the concision," says the apostle—that is, mere mutilators of the body. It is a contemptuous term he uses to designate those who taught that the observance of circumcision was imperative to give one a full standing before God. The apostle will not allow that the mere ordinance is really circumcision. The only true circumcision since the cross is, not a carnal ordinance, but the putting off of the sins of the flesh—the heart-recognition of the fact that the flesh has been put to death in the cross of Christ. It is only as the soul enters into this and uses the sharp knife of self-judgment upon the flesh that one is delivered from its power.

The mere externalists, including legalists and ritualists of all descriptions, always make more of ordinances and outward forms than of the condition of the soul and the spiritual truths symbolized by those ordinances. In Israel we may see this in the fullest way. They boasted themselves of their connection with the temple of the Lord and gloried in ordinances and legal observances, while actually far from God and under His disapproval. Nor should Christians forget that it is just as possible for believers now to be occupied with ordinances and church position while forgetting the more important things of true piety and self-judgment. Nothing that God has commanded is unimportant. But our Lord said to the Jews of His times concerning their intense regard for ordinances and neglect of justice and mercy, "These ought ye to have done, and not to have left the other undone."

In the third verse, we have four distinct statements made, which we do well to consider in detail.

First, "we are the circumcision," that is, we are those who have accepted by faith the end of all flesh in the cross of Christ. We recognize its utter corruption and its powerlessness for service to God, even though placed under the most careful training and supervision. We have, therefore, put it off in the cross of Christ, "Where there is neither Greek nor Jew, circumcision nor uncircumcision, Barbarian, Scythian, bond nor free: but Christ is all, and in all" (Col. 3:11). We began with God by accepting the mark of judgment upon the flesh. We do not now look for anything good in it, but triumph only in Christ.

Second, we "worship God in the spirit." The worship of the old dispensation was largely of a ritualistic character, but the Lord Jesus told the Samaritan woman, "The hour [is coming], and now is, when the true worshippers shall worship the Father in spirit and in truth." Outward forms and services, music and genuflections, do not constitute worship. They may even be hindrances to it. Real worship is that of the heart, when the Spirit of God takes of the things of Christ and shows them unto us. As we are occupied with Him, true praise and adoration ascend to the Father.

Third, we "rejoice in Christ Jesus." Our boast is in the Lord. We are, ourselves, utterly unprofitable, having nothing about us to commend us to Him who, in grace, has saved us. All our boast is in His loving-kindness and His mighty power exercised in mercy on our behalf.

Lastly, he adds, we "have no confidence in the flesh." The flesh of the believer is no more to be trusted than the flesh of the vilest sinner. Regeneration is not a changing of flesh into spirit, nor is that sanctification in which we stand before God a gradual process of such a change within us. "That which is born of the flesh is flesh, and that which is born of the Spirit is spirit." The fleshly nature is never improved, and the new nature received in new birth does not require improvement. "The carnal mind . . . is not subject to the law of God, neither indeed can be." And the spiritual mind is the mind of Christ. It is as we walk in the Spirit that we are delivered from the desires of the flesh. But even after years of godly living, the flesh itself is not one whit better than it was at the very beginning of our Christian life. Therefore, we dare not trust it, knowing that, however blessed the work of God is in our souls, "in [our] flesh . . . dwelleth no good thing."

CHAPTER 14

SELF-CONFIDENCE SET ASIDE FOR CHRIST

Philippians 3:4–7

Though I might also have confidence in the flesh. If any other man thinketh that he hath whereof he might trust in the flesh, I more: circumcised the eighth day, of the stock of Israel, of the tribe of Benjamin, an Hebrew of the Hebrews; as touching the law, a Pharisee; concerning zeal, persecuting the church; touching the righteousness which is in the law, blameless. But what things were gain to me, those I counted loss for Christ. (vv. 4–7)

Paul's own experience comes in aptly to enforce the expression used in verse 3, as to which we have been speaking. He had learned experimentally the utter unprofitableness of the flesh. Looked at from a human standpoint, he had far more to glory in before he was converted to Christ than any of the "concision" among the Philippians could possibly have even afterward. If any had ground for confidence in the flesh, or thought he had, Paul could say, "I more." For they, to whom he wrote, were Gentiles according to natural birth, and, therefore, strangers to the covenants of promise, aliens, and without the true God in the world.

But it was otherwise with the apostle. He was born within the circle of the covenant. He bore upon his body the mark that he was within the sphere of the Abrahamic promise—he was circumcised on the eighth day and, thus, marked off from the Gentile world. Nor were his parents "proselytes of the gate," as Gentiles were called who had forsaken idolatry, and, turning to the God of Abraham, Isaac, and Jacob, had come within the blessings of the covenant through this rite. He, Paul, was of the stock of Israel. For generations back his family had belonged to the covenant people. Then, too, he was descended, not from a bond-woman but from the favorite wife of Jacob. Moreover, when the ten tribes revolted and turned away from the house of David, the particular tribe from which he sprung, that of Benjamin, had remained true to Jehovah's center and loyal to the true kingly line. For though Benjamin had failed grievously in the days of the Judges, so that they were like to have been exterminated out of Israel, yet afterward, through enabling grace, they remained steadfast in the face of grave departure and, thus, won for themselves an immortal name. To be a Benjamite was something in which the flesh might well pride itself.

And as to positive religious conviction, Saul of Tarsus had been a Hebrew of the Hebrews. He was no mere Jew by birth, as some who are indifferent to their Hebrew faith. To the very core of his being he was a follower of the first Hebrew, Abraham himself. As touching the law, he was in practice, faith, and name, a Pharisee. Of the various Jewish sects existing in his day, the Pharisees were the most intensely orthodox and clung most tenaciously not only to the revealed Word of God, but to a vast body of human traditions that had been handed down from their forefathers, and had become in their eyes as sacred as the written Word itself. It is true that our Lord describes many of them as hypocrites, but on the other hand, when He wishes to emphasize the need of positive righteousness, He says, "Except your righteousness . . . exceed [that] of the scribes and Pharisees, ye shall in no wise enter into the kingdom of heaven." He would not have thus spoken if it were not well known that the Pharisees insisted on obedience to the law of God; and Paul himself said, on another occasion, "After the most straitest sect of our religion, I lived a Pharisee." He lived what he professed, and that was Judaism of the strictest kind.

His zeal for the traditions of the elders was seen in the fact that he was a relentless persecutor of the newly born assembly of God. "Exceedingly mad against them," as he himself confessed, he "persecuted them unto strange cities," and even "compelled them to blaspheme." Yet there is no evidence that he was naturally a man of fierce and implacable disposition. In fact, the words of the glorified Lord, "It is hard for thee to kick against the [goads]," would seem to imply the contrary.[1] What he did, he did from a stern sense of duty, not as the fulfillment of his natural desires. Touching the righteousness which the law demanded, he was outwardly blameless. He tells us in Romans 7 that of all the commandments there was only one which really convicted him of sin, and the violation of that one commandment there was no external way of detecting. Who that looked upon the stalwart champion of Jewish orthodoxy could see the covetousness that was in his heart? His outward life gave no evidence of it. Therefore he could speak of himself as blameless.

But when this religious bigot, this stern unyielding champion of what he believed to be the truth of God, was brought into contact with the glorified Christ—that never-to-be-forgotten day on the Damascus turnpike—he realized in one moment the fact declared by the prophet that "all our righteousnesses are as *filthy rags*" (emphasis added). And these things which were gain to him—these things on which he had been building his hopes for eternity—these things which gave him a standing before the eyes of his fellows and caused them to look upon him with admiration, he now saw in their true light—as utterly worthless and polluted garments, unfit to cover him before the eyes of a holy God and deserving only to be cast away. Therefore he exclaims, "What things were gain to me, those I counted loss for Christ."

Let it be carefully noted that he did not count them loss merely for Christianity. In other words, he was not simply exchanging one religion for another; it was not one system of rites and ceremonies giving place to a superior system; or one set of doctrines, rules, and regulations making way for a better one. Often this has been all that conversion has meant. Many people have thought that "changing their religion" was all that God required of them. But it was otherwise with Saul. He had come into actual contact with a divine Person, the once crucified, but now glorified, Christ of God. He had been won by that Person forever, and for His sake he counted all else but loss. If any fall short of this, they are missing entirely the point here emphasized. Christ, and Christ alone, meets every need of the soul. His work has satisfied God, and it satisfies the one who trusts in Him. By resting in Christ, confidence in the flesh is forever at an end. All confidence is in Him who died and rose again, and who "ever liveth to make intercession for [us]."

CHAPTER 15

PAUL'S STEADFAST PURPOSE

Philippians 3:8–11

Yea doubtless, and I count all things [to be] loss for the excellency of the
knowledge of Christ Jesus my Lord: for whom I have suffered the loss of
all things, and do count them but [refuse], that I may win Christ, and be
found in him, not having mine own righteousness, which is of the law,
but that which is through the faith of Christ, the righteousness which is
of God by faith: that I may know him, and the power of his resurrection,
and the fellowship of his sufferings, being made conformable unto his
death; if by any means I might attain unto the out-resurrection from
among the dead. (vv. 8–11, last part literal rendering)

It should be noted that many years of faithful witness bearing intervene be
tween verse 7, which closed our last section, and verse 8, which opens this.
Not only had Paul counted all things but loss for Christ when first he saw His
glory on the road to Damascus, but the long arduous years since had brought in
no change as to this. He still counted all things to be of no worth as compared
with that which had so dazzled the vision of his soul—the excellency of the
knowledge of Christ Jesus the Lord. How different it is with many: fervent and
self-sacrificing in their first love, how soon the fine gold of their devotedness

becomes dimmed and their early freshness passes away! The world, which once seemed so worthless in view of the matchless glory shining in the face of the Savior, begins again to exercise attractive power when the heart has "begun to wax wanton against Christ." It was blessedly otherwise with our apostle. Never for one moment did he go back on the great renunciation he had made when first won for that exalted Jesus whom he had ignorantly persecuted.

And so in this section of the epistle he reaffirms the faith with which he began. He still counted all that earth could offer as dross and refuse when placed alongside of Christ's surpassing glory, which was the one great object ever before him. And this was not with him mere mystical rhapsodizing, for already had he suffered the loss of all things, even of liberty itself, as we know (though in these verses he does not refer to it), and this was all in accord with the dominant purpose of his life, that he might win Christ and be found in Him in the great consummation.

It is not that he is putting the "being found in Christ" on the ground of attainment, or as something to be earned by self-abnegation, but he is letting us into the secret of the supreme emotion of his being. It is as though he were saying, "Ever since I saw Christ in the glory of God I have considered nothing else as worth living for. He has so won my heart that nothing now counts with me but the blessedness of knowing Him, of being completely identified with Him both in life and in death, yea, and beyond death. I would not stand before God in a righteousness of my own now if I could. I desire only to be found in Him. I long only to know Him more intimately, let the suffering involved be what it may. I would even die as He died at last, if need be—any way that He may choose, that at last, whatever way may lead me to it, I shall attain to the great rapture of all saints at His coming, the glorious out-resurrection from among the dead. This for me will be the goal attained which has been for so long before my soul. For then I shall be so completely identified with Him who has won my heart to Himself, that I shall be like Him forever, and with Him through all the ages to come."

I have sought thus to paraphrase his words in order that it may be clearly seen that there is here no element of uncertainty involved in them, as many have supposed and some have taught. He did not fear that he might miss the first resurrection through unfaithfulness or lack of watchfulness. Nor was this out-resurrection from among the dead a matter of present experience (as the verses following show), but refers to that one great event for which every instructed Christian should wait with eagerness—the coming of the Lord Jesus Christ and our gathering together unto Him.

To teach that the rapture is only for certain devoted saints, and that even

Paul himself was haunted with the fear that he would come short of it, would be to lose entirely the sense of the rich grace of God, which is to work in us that glorious change which will make us like Him for whom we wait. The uniform teaching of the apostle is that "they that are Christ's" shall rise "at his coming." And in this hope the aged prisoner of the Lord faced the prospect of martyrdom in its most cruel form. It would be but the appointed means by which he should attain unto the blessedness of the first resurrection.

Nor, it seems to me, can we with propriety say that what the apostle has in mind is the power of resurrection life working in him here on earth so that he may live in the first-resurrection experience, as some have designated it. This would be dangerously near to the "death to nature" theories promulgated by earnest but misled men in the last century, and which resulted in grave departures from sobriety and scriptural order. None had more fully entered into that knowledge of "the power of his resurrection" in his human body than did the apostle, yet he puts the having part in the out-resurrection as the climax of all his years of devoted service. Everything would be incomplete without that. Nor do I know of any other place in the Word of God where the expression is used as referring to a believer's experience. In fact, there is added here a second preposition to intensify the thought of a selective resurrection, otherwise it is the regular expression which distinguishes the first resurrection from the second, which brings up the remaining dead for judgment (Rev. 20:4–5).

That there are two resurrections[1]—not one general rising of saved and unsaved at one time—I take it for granted is clear to my readers, as so much has been written and orally taught upon this subject in recent years. The resurrection of the just; the resurrection of life; the first resurrection; the resurrection from, or out of, the dead—these are all terms synonymous with the one the apostle uses here.

It is with the eye and heart set upon this that the apostle can cast aside as so much *impedimenta* all that would cause him to glory in the flesh or give others an occasion to glory on his behalf. Like the racer stripped for the contest, he struggles ardently on with his eye upon the goal, which is for him this out-resurrection. In view of it, suffering cannot daunt him nor death terrorize him. He sees in both but an opportunity for fuller, sweeter fellowship with his Lord. He would count it all joy to drink of His cup of suffering and to share in His baptism of death—the last of course only as witness bearer, as was promised to James and John before him.

How little do most of us enter into this holy "fellowship of his sufferings!" It is to be feared that some who make greatest pretension as to fellowship in things ecclesiastical would be found sadly wanting when opportunity is given to enter into this fellowship of sorrow and of pain, in which, as in no other phase of fellowship, the soul enters into communion with Him who was on earth a Man of Sorrows and acquainted with grief.

CHAPTER 16

PERFECTION IN TWO ASPECTS

Philippians 3:12–16

Not as though I had already attained, either were already perfect but I follow after, if that I may apprehend that for which also I am apprehended of Christ Jesus. Brethren, I count not myself to have apprehended: but this one thing I do, forgetting those things which are behind, and reaching forth unto those things which are before, I press toward the mark for the prize of the high calling of God in Christ Jesus. Let us therefore, as many as be perfect, be thus minded: and if in any thing ye be otherwise minded, God shall reveal even this unto you. Nevertheless, whereto we have already attained, let us walk by the same rule, let us mind the same thing. (vv. 12–16)

Very early in the history of the church men arose who confounded certain spiritual experiences, real or fancied, with the teaching of the Lord Himself and His apostles in regard to the first resurrection. We know of two by name, Hymenseus and Philetus, of whom Paul wrote to Timothy that they had erred concerning the truth, "saying that the resurrection is past already," and by this overthrew the faith of some. Nothing is more detrimental to Christian testimony than making high claims which cannot be substantiated by experience—as some who take the ground of sinlessness, or of the eradication of an evil nature, because their teachers instructed them that this is their privilege as Christians. If after-experience proves that it is impossible to maintain this practically, there is grave danger that they will become utterly disheartened, and possibly renounce the faith entirely, unless preserved by divine grace.

The apostle, therefore, is careful to make it clear that he did not claim to have reached a state of resurrection perfectness while here upon earth. He uses a word, in this instance, which means completeness, that to which nothing can be added. This state, he declares, he had not already attained. But he had it in view, for he knew that, at the coming of the Lord Jesus Christ, he would be made like Himself, and thus forever free from all tendency to sin. Meantime, he could but follow after, seeking earnestly to lay hold of that for which Christ Jesus had laid hold of him, and in a devoted life to exemplify the power of Christ's resurrection in which he shared. Verses 13–14 might, perhaps, better be rendered as follows: "Brethren, I count not myself to have apprehended; but this one thing, forgetting those things which are behind and reaching forth unto those things which are before, I press toward the mark for the prize of the calling of God on high in Christ Jesus." What he says is that there is only one thing he professes to have apprehended, or laid hold of, namely, that the path of blessing is found in forgetting the things that are past, and seeking to lay hold, practically, of his portion in Christ from day to day while ever keeping the goal in view. To do this is to "follow holiness, apart from which no man shall see the Lord." It is a great mistake to teach that this verse means that unless one attains to certain experiences in holy living he will be forever debarred from a sight of the Lord. It impresses the fact upon us, rather, that he who will see the Lord is one who follows that which characterized his Master here—an inward and outward separation from all that is contrary to the mind of God.

The calling of God on high is that heavenly calling which is characteristic of the present dispensation of grace. Christ is no longer on earth. His world kingdom has not yet been set up. But believers are linked with Him as the glorified Man at God's right hand, and they are called to represent Him in this scene. The prize is the reward conferred by His own hand at the end of the race, and toward this Paul was pressing on, counting as dross and refuse all that would hinder his progress.

To his fellow believers he says, "Let us therefore, as many as be perfect, be thus minded." Are we then to understand that there is real or implied contradiction here to what has gone before? He has told us that he was not perfect. Here he speaks as though he were and links others with him in this perfection. The fact is a somewhat different word is here used from that of verse 12. It implies perfection in growth—in development. An apple in June may be a perfect apple, so far, but it will have much greater completeness, or perfection in that sense, in August or September. And so with the believer.

The perfection of verse 15 is that of full growth, answering somewhat, if not altogether, to the "fathers" of 1 John 2. Such have eschewed the world and its follies. Christ has become to them the one Object before the soul. To live for Him and seek His glory is the only thing that counts in their estimation. And yet such saints are still compassed with infirmity. They are likely to err in judgment. They may make grave mistakes and come to wrong conclusions—influenced as we are by early education, by environment, by mental capacity—and may even be misled as to doctrinal questions. Nevertheless, theirs is the mind of Christ, and they may be comforted by the added words of the apostle that, "If in any thing ye be otherwise minded, God shall reveal even this unto you."

Where there is a willingness to be taught of God, the illuminating grace of the Holy Spirit can be depended upon to open up His Word and guide into all truth. But he would be a bold man indeed, who would dare to say, "I understand all truth, all mysteries are clear to me. I have a perfect apprehension of the divine revelation." Only the boldest egotism could lead anyone to take such ground. How patient, therefore, we need to be with one another. How ready to confess that we know but in part and to recognize the fact that we are ever in need of further instruction. "Nevertheless, whereto we have already attained, let us walk by the same rule, let us mind the same thing." There are truths and principles so plainly put in God's Word that any Spirit-taught believer may readily see them.

Where these truths are learned, it is our responsibility to walk in them—walk together in them, as far as possible, counting on God to reveal to us whatever may be lacking, as we patiently and prayerfully learn from Him through His Word. A wider recognition of these things would lead to more kindly consideration of one another and tend to make us helpers of each other's faith, rather than judges of a brother's doubtful thoughts.

CHAPTER 17

ENEMIES OF THE CROSS OF CHRIST

Philippians 3:17–19

Brethren, be followers together of me, and mark them which walk so as ye have us for an example. (For many walk, of whom I have told you often, and now tell you even weeping, that they are the enemies of the cross of Christ: whose end is destruction, whose God is their belly, and whose glory is in their shame, who mind earthly things.) (vv. 17–19)

The sentence is incomplete and needs the verses that follow to conclude it properly. But I have purposely left it so that we may consider this portion of it the more carefully, for the next part has to do with another and altogether happier theme. Here, the apostle is occupying us with the responsibilities and snares of the pilgrim path. There, he points us on to the goal when all danger will be forever past and with it all opportunity to bear faithful testimony to a rejected Lord in a scene of contrariety. How it behooves us to consider the brevity of the time allotted us for witness bearing! It will soon be forever too late to suffer for and with Christ, and this necessarily means too late to win an honored place in the everlasting kingdom of our Savior God. That which we call *time* is the training school for the ages to come. What a mistake to fritter away its precious moments—so few at the most, as compared with the eternal ages—in things that are of no lasting profit.

Paul was an example both in life and doctrine for all who should come after him. It was not a prideful egotism that led him to plead with saints to follow him and his faithful companions as they followed Christ. He lived what he taught. His life was the practical exemplification of his teaching. He was not one man on the platform or in the meeting, and another in private or in business life. For we need to remember that Paul was no gentleman of leisure. He was not a clergyman afraid to soil his hands with honest labor. He wrought night and day tent-making, when funds were low or when he felt the need of setting an example of activity to any inclined to slothfulness. Yet all the while preaching and teaching publicly and from house to house with a diligence that few if any have equaled, and none have surpassed. He was careful also as to his personal communion with the Lord, striving to keep a conscience ever void of offense toward both God and man. What an example for us all to follow!

That he could not please everybody, even his own brethren, at all times, goes without saying. His work was belittled, his appearance ridiculed, his apostleship denied, and his integrity called in question. There were those who even intimated that he was a crafty deceiver who, by an appearance of frankness, caught with guile the unwary, and at times did evil that good might come! All these charges and insinuations he indignantly refutes in various parts of his writings, while never allowing calumnies to embitter him. He did not return railing for railing, or seek to injure those who would so willingly have injured him. He kept on the even tenor of his way, living Christ and preaching Christ with unchanged ardor to the very end. His wondrous life stood as an abiding answer to those who would malign him. Therefore he could say, "Be followers together of me," and he could consistently call upon the saints to mark his ways and to walk in the same paths.

And though centuries have rolled by since wicked men sought to dishonor him, and the executioner's axe severed his hoary head from his body by Caesar's order, thus finishing his testimony in laying down his life for his Master's sake, he still remains the preeminent example of what the Christian should be, sustained by grace divine while passing through this valley of death's shadow. Let us examine our own ways and see how they measure up to his—not excusing ourselves for failure on the score that times and conditions have changed from those that surrounded him. The same One who wrought effectually in him so long ago will work in us today if there be but a willing mind and a sanctified determination to take his path of unworldliness and devotion to Christ.

Of an altogether different class the next two verses warn us. Many there were, then as now, who, while professing to be in the pilgrim path walked in a vain show, by word proclaiming themselves Christians but by their actions proving that they were enemies of the cross of Christ. Mark it well: they were not said to be enemies of the blood or of the death of Christ. Their opposition was directed against that which told of His shame and rejection by the world—*His cross*. In that cross Paul gloried. By it he saw himself crucified unto the world and the world unto him. But the world lovers refused this. They desired the benefits of His death while refusing to be identified with His shame. They lived for self-indulgence, yet made a pretense of piety. The expression, "Whose God is their belly," really means that they worshiped themselves. *Belly* is self-gratification; and, alas, how many live for self! And yet it is out of this same self, or person, that, when devoted to Christ, living waters shall flow for the refreshment and blessing of others, as our Lord says in John 7:38. Until self is thus displaced as an object for which to live, and surrendered to God as an instrument to be used by and for Christ, there can be no true pilgrim character.

The apostle declares that for these enemies of the cross the end will be destruction. Consider for a moment the solemnity of this. They lived for self-gratification while in this scene. In the life to come they will be in a condition where the gratification of the smallest desire will be utterly impossible. Our Lord told of one who on earth was clothed in purple and fine linen, and fared sumptuously every day, but when suddenly snatched away from it all by the rude hand of death, he found himself in greatest torment, where not even his anguished prayer for a drop of water to cool his parched tongue could be granted. Such is the destruction awaiting those who live for self, ignoring the claims of the Christ of God. And yet, heedless of all this, they go on in their folly, indifferent alike to the admonitions of Scripture, of conscience, and of the Holy Spirit—indifferent also to the warnings and entreaties of men of God who, like Paul, have chosen the better part, and know whereof they speak.

Casting to the winds all godly counsel and sound advice, like flamboyant fools sporting on the edge of a moral precipice, displaying their heedlessness and folly before all, they glory in their shame, and exult in that which might well cause them to bow in penitent grief before redeeming mercy. Unlike Mary, who chose that good part never to be taken from her, or like Moses, who chose to suffer affliction with the people of God rather than enjoy the pleasures of sin for a season, they deliberately reject the good and choose the evil. They put away the hope of heaven for a brief season of sensual or sensuous pleasure here on earth. It is all summed up in the four little words—"Who mind earthly things." Despising the heavenly calling, they choose the earthly and become indeed "dwellers upon the earth," only to be exposed to the fierce vials of the wrath of God in the day when He arises to shake terribly the earth. No wonder the apostle wept as he wrote of such and warned them of their peril in pursuing their evil ways.

CHAPTER 18

HEAVENLY CITIZENSHIP

Philippians 3:20–21

For our conversation [or, citizenship] is in heaven; from whence also we look for the [or, a] Saviour, the Lord Jesus Christ: who shall change our vile body [or, this body of our humiliation], that it may be fashioned like unto his glorious body [or, the body of his glory], according to the working whereby he is able even to subdue all things unto himself. (vv. 20–21)

The Greek word *politeuma* here rendered "conversation" means, as is now well-known, commonwealth, citizenship, or it might almost be transliterated "politics," for it involves all three thoughts. The apprehension of its scope, as here used by the apostle, should help the Christian to understand his true relationship and position regarding the affairs of this life and of the earth.

Philippi was, when Paul wrote, a Roman colony. That is, as a mark of special favor, Roman citizenship had been granted to all the free-born citizens of the former Macedonian capital. This was considered a great privilege. It enabled each Philippian, though dwelling in Macedonia, to say proudly, "My citizenship is in Rome." His responsibilities were directly to the Imperial Power. He had to do with the Emperor, not with the provincial government of Macedonia. Now, apply this to the Christian. Saved by matchless grace, though still living in the world, his commonwealth—the government to which he primarily owes allegiance—is in heaven. He is directly subject to the Lord Jesus Christ, and his conduct is to be regulated by His Word. The realization of this, while keeping him free from entangling alliances with the affairs of this world, will not, of course, tend to lawlessness or insubjection to world rulers. A Philippian, subject to imperial authority, would not be a lawbreaker in Macedonia, inasmuch as the same authority to which he owed allegiance had instituted the government of the country in which Philippi was the chief city. And so the apostle tells us elsewhere, "The powers that be are ordained of God," and he commands Christians to be subject in all things to magistrates, as recognizing the divine authority by which they rule.

But one will search in vain the distinctly Christian part of the Bible—namely, the New Testament Epistles—for any hint that Christians were to seek worldly power or dominion during this present age. Their place is that of subjection, not rule, until Christ Himself returns to reign.

The Emperor, to whom the Philippians owed allegiance, dwelt in Rome. Should he appear in Philippi, he would recognize with special honor those whose citizenship was directly linked with the capital of the empire. Our Lord is in heaven, and from there we look to see Him soon descend when He shall openly confess all those whose citizenship is in heaven—confess them before an astonished and affrighted world (see 2 Thess. 1:3–12).

It is now known, as a result of recent archaeological discoveries, that the term *kurios* (the general word for "Lord" in the New Testament) was an imperial title. More than that, this imperial title was never used in reference to the emperors until, through a public ceremony, they were deified, according to pagan conceptions; therefore it was used as a divine title. At the very time that Paul wrote this letter, it was common to address the brutal man who occupied the imperial throne as "our Lord Nero," using the distinctive term just referred to. How marked the contrast when the Christians, often writhing beneath the bitter persecutions of this unspeakably wicked tyrant, looked expectantly toward the heavens for the return of "our Lord Jesus Christ."

At His coming, the first resurrection will take place. The sleeping saints will be raised and living saints will be changed. For "this corruptible must put on incorruption, and this mortal must put on immortality" (1 Cor. 15:53), and our natural bodies will be changed to spiritual bodies. It should be remembered that when our Bible was translated in the seventeenth century, the word *vile* did not necessarily have the thought of evil connected with it. That was *vile* which was lowly or common: so here "our vile body" is really "the body of our humiliation"—the body which links us with the lower creation, a body common to both saint and sinner. At the Lord's return it will be transformed and made like unto the body of His glory. In that resurrection body He came forth from the tomb, was manifested to His disciples, ascended into heaven, appeared to Saul of Tarsus, and in it He shall soon return with glory. The natural body is really a *soulish* body, or soulual, if we may coin the word, and a spiritual body is a body suited to the spirit. It is not that one is material and the other immaterial. For both are material, though the one is of finer substance than "this mortal body" and no longer subject to certain laws by which the natural body is now controlled. In bodies of glory, then, we shall dwell forever in the city to which we even now belong. It is our own, our native country, as children of God, and we shall never really be at home until we are there with our glorified Lord Himself.

The same divine energy that wrought in Him to raise Him from the dead shall still work through Him until He subdues all things to Himself. Then as we learn from 1 Corinthians 15:24–28, He will deliver the kingdom to the Father, that God, in all His fullness—Father, Son, and Holy Spirit—may be all in all forever and fully manifested in Christ Jesus, who remains eternally our Lord and our Head.

PART 4

CHRIST, THE BELIEVER'S STRENGTH, AND THE CONFIDENT MIND

CHAPTER 19

EXHORTATION TO UNITY

Philippians 4:1–3

Therefore, my brethren dearly beloved and longed for, my joy and crown, so stand fast in the Lord, my dearly beloved. I beseech Euodias, and beseech Syntyche, that they be of the same mind in the Lord. And I entreat thee also, true yokefellow, help those women which laboured with me in the gospel, with Clement also, and with other my fellowlabourers, whose names are in the book of life. (vv. 1–3)

The long parenthesis of the third chapter concluded, the apostle again exhorts to steadfastness and unity. It is very evident that there was incipient division of some nature working in the Philippian assembly. It was in order to meet this, as we have already noticed, that the letter was written; but Paul did not immediately put his finger upon the difficulty. Through the three previous chapters he has been ministering that which should prepare the hearts of the offenders for a final word of exhortation. In this section, he calls them by name, and pleads with them not to let self-interest hinder the work of the Lord.

With expressions of deepest affection, he addresses the assembly as a whole. They are his brethren, dearly beloved, for whom he yearns, and who will be, at the judgment seat of Christ, his joy and crown. It will be noticed that this expression is analogous to that of 1 Thessalonians 2:19–20. There, addressing the saints who had been won to Christ through his ministry, he could say, "For what is our hope, or joy, or crown of rejoicing? Are not even ye in the presence of our Lord Jesus Christ at his coming? For ye are our glory and joy." When, as a servant, he stands at the judgment seat of Christ, that which will fill his heart with gladness will be the sight of those for whose eternal blessing he had been used while laboring in this scene. Rutherford beautifully expresses the same thought when, speaking of the town in which he had labored so long, he cries,

> Oh, if one soul from Anwoth
> Meet me at God's right hand,
> My heaven will be two heavens,
> In Immanuel's land.

Then "he that soweth and he that reapeth [will] rejoice together," as each servant shall come bringing in his sheaves, and, looking up into the face of the Lord, will be able to say, "Behold I and the children which God hath given me."

The crown of rejoicing is the soul-winner's garland, composed of those he has won for Christ. Such must ever stand in a more precious relationship to the one who has been used to their conversion than they possibly can to any other. They are his children in the faith; his sons and daughters in Christ Jesus. Their happy progress in the things of God gladdens his heart, and is, in itself, rich reward for his service in their behalf. While, on the other hand, their failure or breakdown by the way, as evidenced by loss of interest in divine things, dissension, worldly ways again taken up, must rend his heart with grief, and also fill him with a certain sense of shame. "Now we live," writes the apostle elsewhere, "if ye stand fast in the Lord." A brother servant, the apostle John, writing to his converts, says, "And now, little children, abide in him; that, when he shall appear, we may have confidence, and not be ashamed before him at his coming" (1 John 2:28). Notice, it is not that *they* may not be ashamed, but "we," that is, those who were instrumental in leading them to Christ.

So it is in view of all this that Paul earnestly exhorts his beloved Philippians to stand fast in the faith. It is always the effort of Satan to hinder the people of God from steadfastly clinging together, and presenting a united front to the enemy. Alas, that his efforts to introduce dissension so readily succeed because of the flesh in us.

And now, without further delay, and in perfect frankness, the apostle speaks directly to the two offenders against unity, whom he had in his mind from the beginning. And yet there is no sternness, no seeking to lord it over their consciences, but he pleads with them, as though Christ Himself were beseeching, and entreats Euodia and Syntyche. They had been earnest laborers in the gospel, but had fallen out with each other, as we say, and they are exhorted to be of the same mind in the Lord. He certainly does not mean by this that they must think alike in everything or see all things from the same standpoint. This can never be while we are in this world. The very possession of mind, which differentiates man from the brutes, of necessity gives occasion for differences of judgment as to many things, and so calls for much patience toward one another.

No two men ever saw the same rainbow. The slightest difference of position gives each a view at a different angle. The formation and contour of the eye itself has to be taken in consideration. One may discern clearly every distinct shade, while the other may be color-blind, and no amount of argument or persuasion will enable the second to see that which is so clear to the first. And so we may even say no two men have ever read the same Bible. Not that there is one book from God for one person and a different one for another, but the difference is in our apprehension of things. We are so influenced by our environment, by our education, or lack of it, that we are prejudiced when we least realize it. Even when we try to be the most open-minded, we are often misled by our impressions and the limitations of our understanding. Therefore, the need of great patience one with the other.

But if what we have been saying is true, how then can we be of one mind? The verse does not end without making that very plain: "I beseech Euodias, and beseech Syntyche," he writes, "that they be of the same mind *in the Lord*" (emphasis added). If both alike have the mind of Christ—which is the lowly mind—if both alike seek to be subject to the Lord, even though there may be differences of judgment as to many things, each will respect the other's viewpoint, and neither will try to force the other's conscience. Thus all occasion for dissension would be at an end. Alas, that we so little realize this and are often so insistent on what seems to us exceedingly important truth, when nothing vital is at stake, while a brother or sister equally honest and earnest may fail to see things as we see them. At the judgment seat of Christ it may be manifested that, after all, they, and not we, were right or perhaps that both were wrong.

I take it that the third verse was spoken by Paul to Epaphroditus personally, who was, I presume, his amanuensis in the writing of this letter. He was about to return to Philippi, having fulfilled his mission, and now, strengthened after his illness, was to be the bearer of this epistle. The apostle entreats him, as a true yokefellow, to help these women upon his return to that unity of mind to which he had been exhorting them. He mentions that they had labored with him in the gospel, with Clement also, and with others of his fellow laborers, whose names though not given here are in the Book of Life. We are not to understand by this that they occupied the public platform or taught in the assembly of God, participating with Paul and Clement and these other laborers in public testimony, for this would contradict the words of the Holy Spirit through the same apostle as preserved for us in 1 Corinthians 14 and in 1 Timothy 2. But there were many ways in which devoted women could serve the Lord in the gospel. In fact, in oriental, as well as in occidental lands, work for women is of tremendous importance. There were many places where a man could not go, where godly women may have free access. And "laboring in the gospel" implies a great deal more than simply speaking from a platform. In fact, it is a question if this latter be not, in many instances at least, the lesser thing, and the individual heart-to-heart work the greater.

It seems clear that Epaphroditus caught the note of inspiration in these personal words to him, and so he embodied them in this letter. We can be thankful to God that they have come down to us, for they give us deeper insight into the working of the spirit of grace in the mind of Paul, and will be valuable to all who seek to serve the Lord until the church's history on earth is ended.

CHAPTER 20

JOY AND PEACE

Philippians 4:4–7

Rejoice in the Lord always: and again I say, Rejoice. Let your moderation be known unto all men. The Lord is at hand. Be careful for nothing; but in every thing by prayer and supplication with thanksgiving let your requests be made known unto God. And the peace of God, which passeth all understanding, shall keep your hearts and minds through Christ Jesus. (vv. 4–7)

In the opening verse of chapter 3 we have already had the exhortation, "Finally, my brethren, rejoice in the Lord." Undoubtedly, the apostle was, so far as his own mind was concerned, just ready to bring his letter to a close. But, as we have already seen, this was not the mind of the Spirit, and, like his brother-apostle, Jude, on another occasion, he was "borne along" to exhort the saints to "earnestly contend for the faith once delivered." Now he again refers to that which was so much upon his heart. He would have the saints always rejoicing in the Lord. Joy and holiness are inseparable. A holy Christian is able to rejoice even when passing through deepest afflictions. But a believer who, through unwatchfulness, has permitted himself to fall into unholy ways loses immediately the joy of the Lord, which is the strength of those who walk in communion with Himself.

The second exhortation is one to which we may well give earnest heed. In the King James Version we read, "Let your moderation be known unto all men." Undoubtedly, moderation is a most commendable Christian virtue, but there is more to the original word than this. It has been rendered by some "yieldingness." This, too, is an excellent translation, so far as it goes, and suggests that resilience of character which many of us sadly lack. Rotherham gives "considerateness," which adds to the thought, and helps us to a better understanding of the mind of the Spirit in this connection. The Revised Version has "forbearance," and in the margin "gentleness." But if we take all these various terms we shall, I think, find them summed up in the very suggestive rendering given years ago by Matthew Arnold, the English critic, who translated the passage, "Let your sweet reasonableness be manifested to all men."

He pointed out the interesting fact that the word here used is unknown in classical Greek, and it was his impression that Paul coined it for the occasion. What a lovely trait is this sweet reasonableness in a Christian! It is the very opposite to that unyielding, harshly dogmatic, self-determined spirit that so often dominates in place of the meekness and gentleness of Christ. "I beseech you, my brethren," wrote Cromwell to the warring theologians of his day, "remember that it is possible you may be wrong." How apt we are to forget this when engaged in discussions as to either doctrines, methods of service, or church principles!

This does not mean that one need be lacking in intensity of conviction or assurance as to the correctness of doctrines, principles, or practices which one believes he has learned from the Word of God. But it does imply a kindly consideration for the judgment of others, who may be equally sincere and equally devoted—and, possibly, even more enlightened. Nothing is ever lost by recognizing this and remembering that we all know *in part*.

How aptly the brief sentence, "The Lord is at hand," comes in, in connection with the preceding exhortation! I take it that the thought is not exactly "The Lord is coming"; it is rather, "The Lord is standing by." He is looking on; He hears every word spoken; He takes note of every action.

> Closer is He than breathing,
> Nearer than hands or feet.

With the realization that He is thus, in the fullest sense, "at hand," though unseen, how quickly would strife and dissension cease, and the forbearance and grace ever manifested in Himself be seen in His followers!

And now we have a wonderful promise based on a third exhortation, this time in connection with prayer. Our Lord Himself has warned against anxious thought, and the Holy Spirit expands His teaching by saying, "In nothing be anxious." But how am I to obey an exhortation like this when troubles are surging around me, and my poor, restless mind will not be at peace? I feel I must tell somebody. My exercises are like those of the psalmist perhaps, who wrote on one occasion, "I am so agitated that I cannot speak" (Ps. 77:4, F. W. Grant's trans.). What, then, shall I do? To whom shall I turn? It is so natural to worry and fret under circumstances such as these; though I tell myself over and over again that nothing is gained thereby, and my trouble only seems to become exaggerated as I try to carry my own burdens.

But the Spirit of God points the way out. He would have me bring everything, the great things and the little things, perplexing conditions and trying circumstances of every character, into the presence of God and leave them there. By prayer and supplication, not forgetting thanksgiving for past and present mercies, He would have me pour out my requests unto God. I may feel that I do not know the mind of the Lord in regard to them, but that need not hinder. I am to make known my "requests," counting on His wisdom to do for me that which is best both for time and eternity. Thus, casting my care upon Him and leaving all in His own blessed hands, the peace of God (that peace which He, Himself, ever enjoys, though storms and darkness may be round about), a peace passing all understanding, shall guard, as with a military garrison, my heart and (blessed truth, if I but enter into it) my thoughts, or "mind," as it is here translated, through Christ Jesus.

But this I cannot do for myself. I may tell myself over and over that I will not worry, will not fret, but my thoughts, like untamed horses with the bit in their teeth, if I may use such an illustration, seem to run away with me. Or, like an attacking army, they crowd into the citadel of my mind and threaten to overwhelm me. But God, Himself, by the Holy Spirit, has engaged to so garrison my mind and so protect my restless heart, that my thoughts shall neither run away with me nor yet overwhelm me. Every thought will be brought into captivity to the obedience of Christ. Thus I shall enjoy the peace of God, a peace beyond all human comprehension, as I leave my burdens where faith delights to cast every care at the feet of Him who, having not withheld His own Son, has now declared that through Him He will freely give me all things. In this I can rest, for He cannot deny Himself.

CHAPTER 21

EXHORTATIONS

Philippians 4:8–9

Finally, brethren, whatsoever things are true, whatsoever things are honest, whatsoever things are just, whatsoever things are pure, whatsoever things are lovely, whatsoever things are of good report; if there be any virtue, and if there be any praise, think on these things. Those things, which ye have both learned, and received, and heard, and seen in me, do: and the God of peace shall be with you. (vv. 8–9)

These verses conclude the instructions of the apostle. All that follows being in the nature of a postscript—and, while of deep practical value, not directly addressed to saints as homiletical teaching.

Having throughout the epistle put Christ before his readers in so many different aspects, the apostle now sums all up in this brief exhortation to think on things holy, thus recognizing the Old Testament principle, "As a man thinketh in his heart, so is he." Many have missed the very point, however, which it seems clear he is pressing, by taking all these things in an abstract way. It will be found exceedingly difficult to think on things true, honest, just, pure, and lovely, if there be not some definite, concrete example before the mind. Mere occupation with beautiful sentiments and poetic ideals is not, I take it, what he would here inculcate. But all are found fully exemplified in our Lord Jesus Christ as the perfect Man here on earth, and, in measure, these qualities are reproduced by the Holy Spirit in all who have been made partakers of the divine nature. In a certain sense we may think of these words as linking with the exhortation already given to Euodia and Syntyche, who needed to see in each other what the Spirit had wrought.

Let Euodia look coldly and critically upon Syntyche, and occupy her mind with whatever she can find in her character or ways that is contrary to the virtues here mentioned, and the breach between them will be immeasurably widened. Let Syntyche retort by exaggerating every defect or shortcoming in her sister in Christ, and she will soon become so alienated from her that reconciliation will be almost impossible.

But, on the other hand, if Euodia, realizing that Syntyche has been redeemed to God by the same precious blood as herself and is indwelt by the same Holy Spirit, determines to think of the virtues or anything worthy of praise in her life and personality—to magnify her graces and minimize her faults, refusing to indulge in unkind criticism—she will be so attracted by what is of Christ in her that she will find herself linked in heart to the one from whom she had previously turned coldly away.

Is not this what we all greatly need in our dealings with each other? In every truly converted soul there are the manifest inwrought virtues of the Spirit of God—things that are honest, just, pure, lovely, and of good report—the activities of the new nature. If we think on these things, instead of dwelling upon the failures to which all are liable, our fellowship one with another will become increasingly precious as the days go by. And even when there is actual cause for blame, if we stop to consider the circumstances that may have led up to that which seems to us so blameworthy, Christian pity and compassion will take the place of criticism and unkind judgment, which cannot help to restore but only serve to drive farther into sin the erring one. "To err is human; to forgive divine." And even a poet of this world has taught us the folly of judging that which the eye cannot see when, in his quaint Scottish way, he has written,

> We only ken the wrang that's dune,
> We ken na' what's resisted.

We may severely blame the wrongdoer for things that have already deeply exercised his heart and conscience, and been long since cleansed away by the washing of water by the Word as applied by the Lord Jesus Himself.

And, of course, in all our ways it is important that we should never permit our minds to feed, like carrion vultures, on the wicked, filthy, and unholy things of the flesh. This is thoroughly natural to the carnal man, and the carnal mind is still in the believer and will be until the day when our bodies of humiliation shall be changed and made like His body of glory. But we are not to permit it to dominate us, since the Holy Spirit dwells in us to control us for Christ. There is so much that is honest, so much that is just or righteous, so much that is pure, so much that is lovely and loveable, so much that is of good report, so much that is virtuous and trustworthy that it were folly to be occupied with the opposites when we might be taken up with positive good.

And, as we meditate on these things, we grow in grace and in the knowledge of our Lord Jesus Christ; for, as we have already noted, all these beautiful traits were fully exemplified in Him, and they have been imparted, in large measure, to each of His servants; probably to none more so than the writer of this epistle. Therefore, without pride, but as an example to the flock of Christ, he can add, "Those things, which ye have both learned, and received, and heard, and seen in me, do." And as thus practically walking, according to the power of the indwelling Spirit, we have the sweet assurance that "the God of peace shall be with you," thus connecting all this with the promise of verse 7 above where we are assured that "the peace of God" shall garrison the minds and hearts of all who cast their every care on Him. Here we learn that the God of peace will walk with those who seek to walk before Him in piety and holiness of mind and ways.

CHAPTER 22

MINISTRY IN TEMPORAL THINGS

Philippians 4:10–23

But I rejoiced in the Lord greatly, that now at the last your care of me hath flourished again; wherein ye were also careful, but ye lacked opportunity. Not that I speak in respect of want: for I have learned, in whatsoever state I am, therewith to be content. I know both how to be abased, and I know how to abound: every where and in all things I am instructed both to be full and to be hungry, both to abound and to suffer need. I can do all things through Christ which strengtheneth me. Notwithstanding ye have well done, that ye did communicate with my affliction. Now ye Philippians know also, that in the beginning of the gospel, when I departed from Macedonia, no church communicated with me as concerning giving and receiving, but ye only. For even in Thessalonica ye sent once and again unto my necessity. Not because I desire a gift: but I desire fruit that may abound to your account. But I have all, and abound: I am full, having received of Epaphroditus the things which were sent from you, an odour of a sweet smell, a sacrifice acceptable, wellpleasing to God. But my God shall supply all your need according to his riches in glory by Christ Jesus. Now unto God and our

Father be glory for ever and ever. Amen. Salute every saint in Christ Jesus. The brethren which are with me greet you. All the saints salute you, chiefly they that are of Caesar's household. The grace of our Lord Jesus Christ be with you all. Amen. (vv. 10–23)

In this, the closing section of the epistle, Paul thanks the assembly at Philippi for the practical way in which they had manifested their fellowship in the gospel. They were not of those who are willing to profit eternally through the gospel ministry, but have very little exercise as to the temporal welfare of the servants of Christ to whom they owe the knowledge of that truth which has made them free. From the beginning of their Christian lives, the Philippian saints had cared, as occasion offered, for the needs of the apostle, even sending to him of their substance when he was laboring in Thessalonica where he and his companions had gone after being released from the Philippian jail. But years had elapsed since then, and Paul had traveled far and passed through many varied experiences, often finding it quite impossible to keep in close touch with the different assemblies he had been used of God to establish. Consequently it was not strange that, at times, it should seem as if his dearest friends had forgotten him. Nevertheless, the love was there though they had lacked opportunity to display it. But now they had learned of his circumstances as a prisoner in Rome for the truth's sake, and they had hastened to show their fellowship with him in his sufferings by sending Epaphroditus with a gift of love, as we have already noticed.

In acknowledging this, Paul takes occasion to glorify God for His care of him, even when Christian assemblies forgot their indebtedness to him. He had indeed known cold neglect and indifference, but it never soured his spirit nor led him to complain. He noted the cold-heartedness, but he did not find fault. He left it all with the Lord and committed his own circumstances to Him, assured that He never forgot and was never an unconcerned spectator of His servant's sufferings. So, he accepted it all as a course in the school of God, and he could say, "I have learned in whatsoever state I am to be content." The Lord was his portion, and he could rest in the knowledge of His unchanging love and care.

It was not in a moment that he entered into this. He, like all disciples in God's school, had to advance in the life of faith by learning practically the things he could now teach to others. But he had taken his degree, so to speak, and he could now declare, "I know both how to be abased, and know how to abound: every where and in all things I [possess the secret, or I have been initiated] both to be full and to be hungry, both to abound and to suffer need." Blessed lessons these!

And we may say the soul is never really at rest in regard to the trials and testings of the way until these precious secrets have been apprehended.

John Wesley is reported to have said that he did not know which dishonored God the most—to worry, which is really to doubt His love and care, or to curse and swear. Yet every saint would shrink from the latter with abhorrence, while many of us have no sense of the wrong we do when we fret and worry. To rest in faith upon the knowledge that "all things work together for good to them that love God, to them who are the called according to his purpose," should ever be our attitude. And in a very special sense they who minister in word and doctrine (in entire dependence on the One who has sent them out as His ambassadors) are called upon to exemplify this in their calm dependence upon Him whom they serve.

This leads me to say something upon the New Testament principle for the support of those who labor entirely in spiritual things. And, first, let it be noted carefully, there is no such thing known in Scripture as putting the servant of God upon the low level of a salary basis. The only man mentioned in the Bible to be hired by the year as a "minister" was the recreant Levite who was engaged by Micah of Mount Ephraim, and later by the Danites to be their "father and priest" (Judg. 17–18). Even in the legal dispensation, Jehovah Himself was the portion of the Levites. They were prospered and cared for in accordance with the measure in which God blessed His people and their hearts responded to His goodness. In the Christian economy we have no special clerical or extra-priestly class to be supported as professional men by their so-called lay-brethren. The distinction of clergy and laity is utterly unscriptural, and is but part of the Judaizing system that has so perverted the truth of the church. But there are those who are specially gifted as evangelists, pastors, and teachers, and who, in many instances, though not in all, are called upon to separate themselves from secular pursuits in order to give their time unhinderedly to spiritual service. These of old "for his name's sake . . . went forth," we are told in 3 John, "taking nothing of the Gentiles." They were cast entirely on the Lord, and He cared for them through His own grateful people, according to the Word, "Let him that is taught in the word communicate unto him that teacheth in all good things." And so John, by the Spirit, writes, "We therefore ought to receive such that we might be fellow helpers to the truth." Such servants have a claim upon the people of God, not because they are official ministers, but because they are engaged in making known the truth, and in this service all believers are privileged to share. But observe carefully—the servant is never to look to the saints for his support, but to count directly on the Lord and make his personal needs known only to

Him. He need not fear to acquaint the assemblies with special opportunities for ministry to others as occasions arise. Paul did this frequently and earnestly. But rather than mention his personal needs, he would labor with his own hands. Nor did he feel he was degrading his calling in so doing, that thus he might provide things honest in the sight of all men and set an example to any who might be inclined to seek an easy path and depend upon support by those in better circumstances than themselves.

And so the principle is clear: the servant of Christ is to go forth in absolute dependence upon the One who has commissioned him and who makes Himself responsible to meet his needs. But the people of God are called upon to be exercised before Him as to what share they should have in the support of those who are thus engaged. No ministering brother has the right or authority to demand support from the saints. They, not he, must judge whether he is worthy of that support. But, on the other hand, if receiving from him in spiritual things, it is, we are told, a small matter that he should reap their carnal things. "They which preach the gospel should live of the gospel" (1 Cor. 9:14).

For a servant of the Lord to be finding fault because of the smallness of his support is to make manifest at once that his dependence is upon man rather than on God. For saints to be callously indifferent to the temporal needs of those whom they recognize as God-sent messengers is to show themselves out of touch with Him who has given to them the privilege of being in this way fellow helpers to the truth. Thus should both those who minister and those who are ministered to be exercised before God as to their mutual responsibilities.

This had been the path in which Paul had walked for many years, and as he looked back over the journey and saw how he had been sustained of God, he knew he could count on Him for the future. So he faced the days to come with the assurance that he could do all things through Christ who was his strength. He who was to him life, example, and object was also his unfailing source of supply for every emergency that might arise, even to a martyr's death.

But while he did not look to man for his supplies, he shows himself truly grateful for the ministry extended to him. He would not take the gift of love sent by his dear Philippian children in the faith as though it were a mere matter of course. He expresses himself in most appreciative terms as he thanks them for their fellowship, and in this he is an example to all Christ's servants, some of whom have been only too neglectful of the finer courtesies, which often mean more to the saints than they realize.

Paul received the gift not because he desired to profit by means of their generosity, but because he saw in it an added evidence of the working of the spirit of grace in their souls, and this was for their blessing, as well as relieving his need. And so he gladly accepted it all, seeing in it "an odour of a sweet smell, a sacrifice acceptable, wellpleasing to God."

Nor would He, for whose glory they ministered the gift to His imprisoned servant, allow them to put Him in their debt, but engaged Himself to supply all their need, according to His riches in glory through Christ Jesus. The more blessed part must always be His, for when we have given to our utmost limit, we have only returned Him a little of His own, and even that He will abundantly repay.

The last three verses give the concluding salutation. Note again how "every saint" is affectionately greeted. He would refuse to the last to recognize any parties among them. And all with him joined in saluting them—particularly some, evidently newly come to the faith, and possibly as a result of coming in contact with him in his prison cell, whom he mentions as "those of Caesar's household," who belonged to the imperial guard.

And so we close our meditations on this instructive epistle with a message of "grace" ringing in our souls.

COLOSSIANS

PREFACE

Expositions of Colossians abound, many of them of great value, yet each generation seems to call for fresh and new applications of divine truth. Hence this volume.

These lectures have been delivered at many Bible conferences throughout the United States and Canada, and are issued in book form in response to the earnest requests of many who heard them. If read with the open Bible beside them, and thus used not as a substitute for, but as an aid to, the study of the Word itself, it is hoped they may prove helpful to a wider circle of students of the Book of books.

The times are solemn. Old errors are being paraded in new terms, on all sides. Therefore the need of a new examination of this great epistle that so effectively meets the philosophical, mystical, and legalistic speculations of carnal men. May God be pleased to bless these lectures to that end!

—H. A. IRONSIDE

PART 1

DOCTRINAL

CHAPTER 1

GENERAL CONSIDERATIONS
AND ANALYSIS

No one familiar with the Pauline Letters can fail to see how intimately linked
are those to the Ephesians and the Colossians. It is very likely that the letter
from Laodicea, referred to in the last chapter of the epistle we are considering,
is really our epistle to the Ephesians, and therefore we can understand why the
apostle was anxious that both should be read by the same people. My reasons for
saying this will come out later. Some, in fact, who do not accept the inspiration
of the New Testament have supposed that Colossians was a crude attempt to
rewrite Ephesians from memory, but a careful examination of both letters shows
that the one is the correlative of the other.

Ephesians presents the great truth revealed to Paul and through him made
known to all nations for the obedience of faith, and which he emphatically calls
the mystery. It is the church as the body of Christ in its heavenly aspect, as 1 Corinthians reveals the body in responsibility down here on the earth. Ephesians, of
course, does not overlook the importance of our responsibility to walk according
to the calling wherewith we are called, and to manifest the unity of the Spirit in
our measure while still in this scene. Doctrinally, however, it is the body as the
aggregate of all believers from Pentecost to the rapture, united to a risen Christ
by the indwelling Holy Spirit, that seems the theme of that epistle.

Colossians, on the other hand, has to do with Christ as the Head of the body. It seeks to fix the hearts of the saints upon Him as risen and glorified, known no longer after the flesh but, in resurrection, the Head of a new order, and believers as responsible to manifest Him, to hold the Head, here in this world. So we might say the Headship of Christ is the theme of this epistle. We need not therefore be surprised to find great similarity in Ephesians and Colossians, for so intimate is the link between Christ and the members of His body that what is said of the one may often be said of the other, and it is given to the members of the body to manifest the risen life of the Head. He it is with whom the Holy Spirit occupies us in order that we may be separated practically from all that would dishonor Him and delivered from anything that would tend to keep Him at a distance.

At the beginning there was very real need for such ministry. Christianity as a divine system seemed likely to be overwhelmed (only that the Lord Himself was watching over His own truth) in the first centuries by a strange mixture of Jewish legality, Grecian philosophy, and Oriental mysticism, so interwoven as to form several altogether new systems with which the name of Christ was linked in a most cunning way. The result was the "mystery of iniquity" referred to in 2 Thessalonians 2. These various systems were known under the general name of "Gnosticism." This, of course, in pretension, at least, was the very opposite to what Huxley some years ago designated "Agnosticism." The latter term means "without knowledge."

The Agnostic says God is unknowable, the mystery of the universe is unsolvable. He says, "There may or may not be a personal God back of this universe. Matter may or may not be eternal. Man may or may not survive death. I do not know." He complacently takes it for granted that because he does not know, no one else does. He refuses the divine revelation given us in Holy Scripture and so is content to be an ignoramus (which is but the Latin equivalent for Agnostic), when he might have assured knowledge as one taught of God.

The Gnostic, on the other hand, says, I do know. *Gnosis*, from which the term is derived, simply means "knowledge." *Epignosis*, used by the apostle for Christianity, is really "super-knowledge." The Gnostic professed to have fuller knowledge of the mysteries of life and death and heavenly beings than the Bible itself reveals. He added to, or perverted, the scriptural revelation, linking with it weird Persian dreams and human reasonings. He was neither a Jew, a Christian, a Philosopher, nor a Zoroastrian. He considered himself superior to them all, very much as the Theosophists do today, having taken what he thought to be the best out of all these systems and made a new system therewith. This weird imitation of the divine mysteries pretended to great depth of spirituality, to remarkable fullness of knowledge, to great profundity of thought. It was therefore most attractive to the natural mind, ever delighting in speculation on sacred themes, but it was satanic in origin, and deliberately planned by the enemy to hide the glory shining in the face of Christ Jesus, concerning whom the Gnostics indulged in the wildest speculations. I have neither time nor space here to go into the weird speculations of Gnosticism with its amazing conception of grades of spirit beings mediating between the uncreated God and His creatures. Those who are interested can readily find access to full explanations concerning the Demiurge and the host of Kabalistic Eons and inferior emanations supposedly coming in between the soul and God.

The place that Christ Himself held in this system varied according to the vagaries of the respective teachers. Some thought that Jesus was but a man, and the Christ, the divine Spirit which came to Him at His baptism and which left Him at the cross, so it could not be said Christ died, but simply Jesus died. You will recognize this as the root error of what is commonly called Christian Science and of most phases of the so-called "New Thought" of today. Others held that the body of Jesus was only spiritual, not material. They linked evil with matter and therefore refused to believe that "the Word became flesh."

The first of these systems seems to be before the mind of the apostle Paul in the writing of Colossians. The second is met by the apostle John in his three Epistles. Both systems would rob the saints of the true Christ of God. They put Him afar off with many angels intervening who must first be invoked and placated before union with Christ can be known. Paul shows that we come to Him immediately, He being the one Mediator between God and men, the Man Christ Jesus. Again, these Gnostics placed varied ranks of principalities and powers, glorious spirit beings, above and beyond Him, leading up to the invisible God. Whereas the apostle Paul shows us that He is the Creator of all principalities and powers, and that they must all be subject to Him who is Himself the image of the invisible God.

I would not think it necessary to occupy people with these old errors were it not that the danger of losing sight of the Head is as real today as it was then. Every modern erroneous cult is just some old satanic heresy revived, and each is designed to misrepresent some aspect of revealed truth in regard to Christ and His redemptive work. The advocates of these systems may profess great humility and preach and practice great self-abnegation, even to the neglecting of the body and its physical needs, but they all put Christ Jesus—the true Christ of God—at a distance, and an imaginary Christ, a Christ who is not an atoning Savior, in His place. Some degree of familiarity with the ancient theories might save honest souls from being entangled in the meshes of these newer systems. Therefore the need, in every age, of reading this Colossian letter afresh in order that we ever may hold the Head.

It has been observed by others, but will bear repeating, that so intent is the Spirit upon glorifying Christ in this wonderful epistle that He ever hides Himself. In Ephesians, where it is the truth of the one body that is being unfolded, the Holy Spirit is mentioned many times, and we have clear teaching as to His personality and operations. In Colossians He is never mentioned doctrinally, and only once incidentally, if I may so say where I recognize divine design throughout, and that is in verse 8 of chapter 1 where the writer speaks of having heard through Epaphras of the Colossians' "love in the Spirit." This is surely most significant. Even the Holy Spirit Himself, eternally coequal with the Father and Son, who all together constitute one God, would nevertheless hide Himself if men belittle or lose sight of the Lord Jesus as Head of the new creation. The blessed Paraclete speaks not from or of Himself but He takes of the things of Christ and shows them unto us. He would not even risk (to speak after the manner of men) being put in as one coming between the believer and Christ.

It may be well to point out that so far as we have any record Paul had never been to Colosse as a ministering servant, though Philemon, who was of that assembly, had been converted through him. But the saints in that city he had not seen in the flesh. Many individuals may have heard him during the time he was in Ephesus when "all in Asia" heard the Word, as related in Acts 19. By Asia here we are not to understand either the continent nor yet Asia Minor, but a much smaller district, ruled by a Roman proconsul, and therefore known as the "proconsular province of Asia." Thither Paul was at one time forbidden to go. There he later labored with much blessing. There the seven churches of the Apocalypse were afterward located. Though Colosse was not one of these addressed by the Lord when He appeared to John in Patmos, yet it was situated very close to Laodicea, which with Colosse and Hierapolis formed a trio of cities in which were large Christian assemblies in early days.

Epaphras was the chosen instrument for the evangelization of Colosse. He evidently remained among the saints and cared for them as a godly pastor afterward. But he found himself hard beset by emissaries of Satan, who were bent upon misleading these young believers for their own selfish advantage. He therefore sought the help of Paul, the apostle, who was at this time a prisoner in Rome. It was in response to his plea that the letter was penned by divine inspiration, which is now before us.

Another subject which is full of interest is the fact that God in so many instances permitted error in doctrine or corruption in life in the early churches to be the means of adding to the volume of divine revelation and instruction.

It is a signal mercy that in His wisdom God allowed every possible form of error to arise in the apostolic era of the church's history in order that all might be exposed, and the truth declared through inspired men that thus the faith in its simplicity might be preserved for the generations to come. As a result of this, Satan has nothing new to offer. Old heresies are redressed and brought forward as new conceptions of truth from age to age, but in this respect, "there is nothing new under the sun." Therefore, all the Christian needs to protect him from modern systems of an evil character is a better acquaintance with the Word of God, where the truth is taught in its purity and the lies of the adversary are brought out into the light and fully exposed. No one familiar with the teaching of Colossians, for instance, will ever be misled by the specious sophistries of the various occult systems now being foisted on a credulous public, such as Theosophy or Spiritualism, nor will he be deluded by the revived Gnostic religions of Eddyism, Unity School of Christianity, or other branches of the misnamed New Thought.

In studying any book of the Bible it is well to have its outline clearly in mind. I submit the following synoptic analysis as a suggestive outline of the epistle to the Colossians:

PART 1: DOCTRINAL (1:1–3:4)
  A. Salutation (1:1–2)
  B. Introduction (1:3–8)
  C. Paul's prayer and thanksgiving (1:9–14)
  D. Twofold headship of Christ (1:15–19)
  E. Twofold reconciliation (1:20–22)
  F. Twofold ministry of the present dispensation (1:23–29)
  G. Christ the true wisdom: Revelation of the mystery of God (2:1–7)
  H. Christ the antidote for Agnostic Philosophy (2:8–10)
  I. Christ the antidote for Jewish Legality (2:11–17)
  J. Christ the antidote for Gnostic Mysticism (2:18–19)
  K. Christ the antidote for Carnal Asceticism (2:20–23)
  L. Christ the believer's life and object (3:1–4)

PART 2: PRACTICAL (3:5–4:18)
  A. Practical holiness by conformity to Christ (3:5–17)
  B. Natural relationships sanctified (3:18–4:1)

C. Concluding exhortations (4:2–6)
D. Salutations (4:7–18)

This is, of course, in no sense arbitrary. Many other outlines have been suggested, and some of these may be much better than that which I have suggested. But it is along these lines that I purpose examining afresh this precious portion of the Word of God, which, like all Scripture, is written for our learning, and seems to have increasing value as new cults and false systems abound, all designed to make us lose sight of the Head and forget our union with Him in glory.

CHAPTER 2

THE SALUTATION AND INTRODUCTION

Colossians 1:1–8

Paul, an apostle of Jesus Christ by the will of God, and Timotheus our brother, to the saints and faithful brethren in Christ which are at Colosse: Grace be unto you, and peace, from God our Father and the Lord Jesus Christ. (vv. 1–2)

Thirteen epistles in the New Testament begin with the name Paul. A four teenth letter, concerning the authorship of which there is considerable dispute, is nevertheless generally accepted as from the same pen, namely, the epistle to the Hebrews. But the opening word of that epistle is God. The thirteen beginning with the word Paul are addressed either to churches among the Gentiles or to individual believers who were on full church ground. Paul was the apostle to the Gentiles and as such he magnified his office. He was not the apostle to the Hebrews. If, therefore, he was the one chosen to write that wonderful opening up of the old and new covenants, as I firmly believe, it was quite in keeping with his Gentile apostleship that his name should be hidden. Christ alone was the apostle and prophet of the new covenant, as Moses and Aaron had been of the old, and so the opening word of Hebrews is simply God, but God speaking in His Son.

In this Colossian letter, as in the Philippian epistle, Paul associated Timothy with him in the salutation. The bond between these two men of God, so far apart in age though they were, was a very real one. Timothy was converted during Paul's ministry at Lystra, and on his next visit to the same region the brethren took occasion heartily to commend this young man to him, as one in whom marked spiritual graces were manifest and who gave evidence of considerable gift, and was therefore, in their judgment, suited to go out in the ministry of the Word. Acting on their advice, Paul took Timothy with him in the work after the elder brethren had solemnly laid their hands upon him, commending him to God for this special service. Throughout the years that followed, Timothy had proven himself in every respect reliable and devoted. His unselfish concern for the welfare of the people of God and his loyal attachment to his human leader endeared him very much to the venerable apostle. It would seem that Timothy had even accompanied Paul, or else followed him to Rome, and was either sharing his imprisonment or within easy reach doing what he could to alleviate the suffering of the apostle, as well as ministering among the Roman believers. So he here connects the young preacher with himself when he sends his greetings to the saints at Colosse.

Paul attributed his own apostleship directly to the will of God. It was He who had revealed Christ both to and in him and set him apart for service, commissioning him to proclaim the unsearchable riches of grace among the Gentiles. It would be preposterous to suppose that the laying on of hands of the church at Antioch, as mentioned in Acts 13, conferred any authority whatsoever upon either Barnabas or Paul, inasmuch as they had been approved laborers in the gospel for some time. It simply expressed, as in Timothy's case, the fellowship of the local assembly. It was the Holy Spirit who sent them forth and ordained them. Writing to the Galatians also, Paul uses similar expressions, and declares he is an apostle not of men nor by men. This is a principle of far-reaching importance in connection with the work of the ministry. Whenever men presume to add anything to the divine call or to confer authority on a servant of Christ, they are usurping the place of the Holy Spirit. The most that any "laying on of hands" can do is to express fellowship in the work.

In the second verse the Christians at Colosse are addressed as "the saints and faithful brethren." The first expression suggests the divine call; the second, the human response. It is God who designates His redeemed ones as saints, yet Romanists and many Protestants are generally astray as to the meaning of the term. With the first class, a saint is a particularly holy person who displays great devotion or possesses miraculous powers, and is credited in the calendar of intermediaries with a superabundance of merit or goodness which may be appropriated by others. With many who profess greater enlightenment, a saint is one who has become victorious in the struggle with sin and has been received triumphantly into heaven. So they speak of the Christian dead as "sainted." But the scriptural conception is altogether different. The vilest sinner is constituted by God, a saint, the moment he puts his trust in the Lord Jesus Christ, "who was delivered for our offenses and raised again for our justification." Thus we are saints by calling and not primarily by practice. However, we should be careful not to divorce the practical side of things from the doctrinal. Being saints, we are now responsible to live in a saintly way. In other words, we are to live out practically what God has already declared to be true of us doctrinally. We do not become saints by the display of saintly virtues; but because we are saints we are to cultivate saintly characters. This, of course, is done in communion with God, in obedience to His Word, as we walk in the power of the Holy Spirit.

The second expression, "faithful brethren," does not, I take it, imply any advance upon the first one, nor do the two terms indicate two classes of believers. "Faithful brethren" are really brethren who believe; even as we read elsewhere, "They that be of faith are blessed with faithful Abraham." It might be translated either, "They that have faith are blessed with faithful Abraham," or, "They that believe are blessed with believing Abraham." There is an intentional connection between the two terms. All real Christians, therefore, are believing or faithful brethren. If any profess to be Christ's who do not believe His Word, they but show themselves to be unreal and false to their profession. For it is written, "He that cometh to God must believe that he is, and that he is the rewarder of them that diligently seek him." And again we are told, "If ye continue in my word, then are ye my disciples indeed."

The usual apostolic salutation follows. "Grace be unto you, and peace, from God our Father and the Lord Jesus Christ." Grace is God's free unmerited favor. It is even more than that. It is favor against merit. When we merit the very opposite God lavishes His loving-kindness upon us. That is grace. He who sits upon a throne of grace bids us come boldly to obtain grace and mercy as daily needs arise. What saint can but echo the words in the hymn,

> Since our souls have known His love,
> What mercies has He made us prove?

Peace is here, of course, the peace of God garrisoning His people's hearts in the day of evil. It is peace amid the most disquieting circumstances, because assured that "all things work together for good to them who love God, to them who are the called according to his purpose" (Rom. 8:28).

We pass on, then, to the introduction:

> We give thanks to God and the Father of our Lord Jesus Christ, praying always for you, since we heard of your faith in Christ Jesus, and of the love which ye have to all the saints, for the hope which is laid up for you in heaven, whereof ye heard before in the word of the truth of the gospel; which is come unto you, as it is in all the world; and bringeth forth fruit, as it doth also in you, since the day ye heard of it, and knew the grace of God in truth: as ye also learned of Epaphras our dear fellowservant, who is for you a faithful minister of Christ; who also declared unto us your love in the Spirit. (vv. 3–8)

We are reminded of the introduction to the epistle to the Ephesians as we read these words, which begin with an expression of thanksgiving to the God and Father of our Lord Jesus Christ. This presents God in a double character as Creator and as Savior. It is through Jesus Christ that our salvation is mediated. Having heard of the conversion of the Colossians, the apostle's heart was stirred to prayer on their behalf. He writes, "Praying always for you since we heard." For him to learn of others coming to Christ invariably meant that his burden of prayer was increased. He felt, as few men ever have felt, the great need of intercession for the people of God, for he knew well the fearful opposition of Satan the prince and god of this world toward those who trust in the Lord Jesus Christ. He realized the prevailing power of prayer to defeat the adversary. Therefore he bows in the presence of God in earnest supplication on behalf of those whom grace has saved, and he tells us farther on what it was for which he prayed; so we do not now linger on that.

It is interesting to notice how faith, love, and hope are linked together here as in so many other places in Scripture. The order is different in 1 Corinthians 13. There, where he is exalting love, he puts faith first, hope second, and love last, as that which will abide when the other two have passed away. But here it is hope that closes that life which begins with faith, and the two are linked together by love. Faith lays hold of the cross. Hope looks on to the glory. Love is the power that constrains the saint in view of both.

It was a Divine Person to whom they had trusted their souls. People are troubled sometimes for fear their faith should not be of the right quality, or might prove of insufficient quantity to save them. But it is important to observe that it is not the character nor the amount of faith that saves. It is the Person in whom faith rests. The strongest faith in self-effort, or in the church, or in religious observances would leave the soul forever lost. But the feeblest faith in the Christ who died and rose again saves eternally. Some people try to make a Savior of their faith, but Christ alone is the Savior, and faith is but the hand that reaches out to Him.

Then he speaks of the love that they had to all the saints. This is precious indeed, and is the evidence both of the divine nature imparted in new birth and of the indwelling of the Holy Spirit. It is the very nature of the newborn soul to love not only God, but those who are begotten of Him. This love knows no sectarian limitation but embraces all the people of God.

Hope looks on to the future, so he speaks of the hope which is laid up in heaven and of this they had learned in the word of the truth of the gospel. No one fully appreciates the gospel who leaves out the blessed hope of the Lord's return to receive His people to be with Himself in the Father's house. This is the glad consummation of the believer's life of faith and love and hope. Death is never set before the believer as his hope—but always it is the Lord's return for which he is to wait.

The gospel is God's good news about His Son, and therefore, when fully preached, necessarily includes the proclamation of His true sinless humanity, His Deity, His virgin birth, His vicarious sacrifice, His glorious resurrection, His present session as Advocate and High Priest at God's right hand in heaven, and His coming again to reign in power and righteousness when all His redeemed will be associated with Him. All these precious truths are included in the word of the truth of the gospel.

In verse 6 we learn that this gospel, even in Paul's day, had been carried to the very ends of the earth. The same message that had reached Colosse had been preached in all the world, as verse 23 also declares. And, wherever this great evangel of the cross had gone, it had produced fruit to the praise and glory of God in those who believed it. It is the height of folly to look for fruit before the soul has settled peace, or to expect evidence of salvation in the life before the gospel has been believed. Salvation is altogether of grace. Human effort has no place in it at all. Neither are we saved by the work of the Spirit within us producing that ninefold fruit mentioned in Galatians 5. We are saved by the work of Christ for us, a work done altogether outside of ourselves, and in which we had no part excepting to commit the sins that put the Savior on the cross. An old man expressed it correctly when he said, "I did my part and God did His—I did the sinning, and God did the saving. I took to running away from Him as fast as my sins could carry me, and He took after me until He run me down!" Others might express it more elegantly, but no one could tell it more clearly.

The gospel is a message to be believed, not a collection of precepts or a code of laws to be obeyed. It is of faith that it might be by grace—"not of works, lest any man should boast." But the moment the message is believed it produces new life in the soul, and the Spirit seals the believer by coming to dwell within him. This invariably results in precious fruit for God. And this the Colossian believers had exemplified in their own experiences since they heard and knew the grace of God in truth. Observe that the words in verse 6, *of it*, are better omitted.

It was not through the apostle Paul that the message had been carried to Colosse, as we have already noticed. So far as we know he had never visited that city as a messenger of the cross. He speaks in this letter of those whose faces he had not seen in the flesh. It was another devoted man of God, Epaphras by name, who had proclaimed the gospel to them. Paul speaks of him affectionately as "our dear fellowservant," and he declares that he was a faithful minister of Christ. His outstanding characteristic, as gathered from 4:12, was that of fervency in prayer. How blessed when faithful preaching and fervent prayer go together! Alas, that they are so often divorced!

In verse 8, as we have seen, we get the only reference to the Holy Spirit that is found in this epistle. It has already been remarked that when the truth as to Christ, the Head of the church, is being called in question, or when Satan is seeking to interpose anything between the soul and Christ, God will not even occupy the saints with the person or work of the Spirit, lest by occupation with subjective truth they lose sight of the great objective verities. So here the reference to the Spirit is only incidental. He simply mentions the fact that Epaphras had told Paul and his fellow workers of their love in the Spirit. It was a precious testimony to the happy state of these dear young Christians, so recently brought out of paganism with all its abominations.

Now as a company set apart to the name of the Lord Jesus Christ, they were characterized by that love which the Spirit sheds abroad in the hearts of those who are born of God. This is all-important. To pretend to great zeal for the truth of the one body while failing to manifest the love of the Spirit is to put the emphasis in the wrong place. Doctrinal correctness will never atone for lack of brotherly love. It is far more to God who is Himself love, in His very nature, that His people walk in love one toward another, than that they contend valiantly for set forms of truth, however scriptural. "Truthing in love" (which would correctly convey the thought of Ephesians 4:15) is more than contending for formulas. It is the manifestation of the truth in a life of love to God and to those who are His, as well as for poor lost sinners for whom Christ died.

CHAPTER 3

PAUL'S PRAYER AND THANKSGIVING

Colossians 1:9–14

For this cause we also, since the day we heard it, do not cease to pray for you, and to desire that ye might be filled with the knowledge of his will in all wisdom and spiritual understanding; that ye might walk worthy of the Lord unto all pleasing, being fruitful in every good work, and increasing in the knowledge of God; strengthened with all might, according to his glorious power, unto all patience and longsuffering with joyfulness; giving thanks unto the Father, which hath made us meet to be partakers of the inheritance of the saints in light: who hath delivered us from the power of darkness, and hath translated us into the kingdom of his dear Son: in whom we have redemption through his blood, even the forgiveness of sins. (vv. 9–14)

This section reminds us of the prayers of the apostle for the Ephesians, as recorded in chapters 1 and 3 of that epistle. There is something very precious and exceedingly instructive in being thus permitted to share the thoughts of, and notice the petitions offered up by, the apostle Paul for the Lord's people in various circumstances. His deep concern for their growth in grace, their enlightenment in divine things, their apprehension of the purpose of God, and the manifestation of spiritual power in the life—all these come out very strikingly as he bows his knees before the God and Father of our Lord Jesus Christ. He was not content to know people were justified and hence safe for eternity.

He was controlled by the earnest desire that each one should understand the hope of his calling in order that the life and walk might be in harmony with it, and that they might remember they were here to represent Christ, their risen Head. These are what formed the burden of his prayers. It is questionable if any merely human writer has ever been able to give as helpful suggestions for our own prayer life as will come to us in our meditation upon these various petitions.

In verses 9–11 we have set forth certain blessings for which he prays. In verses 12–14 there are others for which he gives thanks. It is very important to distinguish these things, that is, to have clearly in mind the privileges and blessings which are nonforfeitable because confirmed to us by God in Christ from the moment we believe on Him who died to make them good to us. The additional blessings for which we need to pray daily, and concerning which there should be constant soul-exercise lest we fail to enter into and enjoy them. Many believers fail in not distinguishing the two classes of blessings.

In certain circles almost every public prayer will be concluded somewhat as follows: "We pray Thee, forgive us our sins and wash us in the blood of Jesus. Receive us into Thy kingdom, give us Thy Holy Spirit, and save us at last for Christ's sake, Amen." Yet every petition in this prayer has already been granted to the believer in Christ! God has forgiven us all trespasses. We are cleansed by the blood of Jesus. He has already translated us out of the kingdom of darkness into that of the Son of His love. He has sealed us with His Holy Spirit, for "if any man have not the Spirit of Christ, he is none of His." And we are saved eternally from the moment we believe the gospel. Therefore we might far rather cry exultantly in faith: "We thank Thee that Thou hast forgiven all our sins, and washed us from every stain in the blood of the Lamb. Thou hast brought us into Thy kingdom, given us Thy Holy Spirit, and saved us for eternity."

Faith says "Amen" to what God has declared in His Word to be true. To go on praying for blessings that He tells us are already ours is the most subtle kind of unbelief, and robs us of the enjoyment that should be our portion if we but had faith to lay hold of the exceeding great and precious promises which are ours in Christ.

Let us then follow carefully the apostle's prayer, weighing every phrase and clause. He says, "[I] pray for you, . . . [that] ye might be filled with the knowledge of his will." Those who were troubling the Colossian saints boasted of their superior knowledge. They had evolved a complex system of mystical and wholly imaginative teaching in regard to the soul's approach to God through an interminable number of intermediaries, coupled with ascetic regulations and legal observances. In their eyes the gospel as preached by Paul was simplicity indeed, so much so that they looked upon it as a child's conception of the philosophy of the universe, which was puerile for men of mature minds. But he who knew this gospel in all its grandeur, as few other men have ever known it, speaks here of being "filled with the knowledge of God's will." He uses a superlative in the place of a word which the Gnostics were very fond of. They boasted of *Gnosis*—"knowledge." He says, *Epignosis*, meaning, literally, "super-knowledge." It is in the divine revelation alone that this is found.

By this term, "the knowledge of his will," I do not understand him to be referring merely to God's will for the individual believer's life from day to day (though, indeed, that would be involved in the fuller thought of the will of God, as the drop of water is included in the ocean), but by His will, I take it, he means the wondrous plan or program of the Father known from eternity and now being carried out in time to have its consummation in the ages to come—"the eternal purpose of God." Here is super-knowledge indeed! Here is that which the cleverest human intellect could never fathom, apart from divine revelation. And this revelation we have in our Bibles. It runs throughout the Scriptures from Genesis to the Apocalypse, furnishing a theme for devout contemplation, and demanding enthusiastic study and careful examination by men of the most erudite minds and brilliant intellects, and the deepest investigation of the most spiritual believers. But in which also the unlearned and the ignorant Christians will find constant enjoyment if they but allow themselves to be guided by the Spirit in searching the Scriptures to see whether these things are so.

So the words that follow stress the important fact that truth is not learned through the intellect alone. He prays that they may comprehend these things "in all wisdom and spiritual understanding." Wisdom is the ability to use knowledge aright, and is imparted by the Spirit, and He alone gives true understanding. Therefore, if we would learn the mind of God as revealed in His Word, there must be subjection of heart to the divine Teacher, and that self-judgment and self-distrust which leads one to walk softly before God; not in self-will or egotism, but in humility and lowly dependence on the One who inspired the Holy Scriptures, which alone can make wise the simple.

Then we learn in verse 10 that if God opens up His truth to us it is not merely that we may delight in the wondrous things He has revealed, but it is His desire that we walk in the power of that which He makes known to us. So the prayer goes on, "That ye might walk worthy of the Lord unto all pleasing." We can only walk worthy of the Lord as we know His mind. The study of His Word and a godly walk should ever go together.

It is noteworthy that in Ephesians 4:1 we are exhorted to "walk worthy of [our] vocation," or calling, as members of the body of Christ, while in Philippians 1:27 we are told to walk worthy of the gospel, which we are left in the world to proclaim. Then in 1 Thessalonians 2:12 we are bidden to "walk worthy of God," Himself, who has called us to His kingdom and glory. Our walk is ever to be in accordance with the truth revealed to our souls. So here we are to walk worthy of the Lord, He who is the Head of the new creation to which we now belong.

Dr. Griffith Thomas points out that the word here rendered "pleasing" is not found in any other passage in the New Testament, but is used in Greek elsewhere to mean "a preference of the will of others before our own." Bishop Handley Moule translated the phrase, "Unto every anticipation of His will."

This is blessed indeed, when the will of God is sweeter far than our own will, and we delight in doing as He would have us, not in order to propitiate Him but to give joy to His heart. Yet most of us learn so slowly that the only true happiness in life is to be found in doing the will of God. In vain we seek for satisfaction by trying to have our own way, until at last like a bird, wearied out with flying against the bars of its cage, we fall back upon the will of God and learn that in it the mind and heart find perfect rest.

> Oh, the peace my Saviour gives;
> Peace I never knew before;
> And the way has brighter grown
> Since I've learned to trust Him more.

It is the subject believer who becomes fruitful, so he adds, "being fruitful in every good work." Or it might be better rendered, "bearing fruit in every good work." When we speak of every good work, we are not to think simply of preaching the gospel, teaching the Holy Scriptures, or engaging in what is sometimes called Christian activity or church work. We are very prone to do this and to distinguish between secular employment and sacred. But we need to be reminded over and over again that everything in a believer's life is sacred. The church of Rome distinguishes seven sacraments. But every act of a Christian should have a sacramental character using the word as generally understood. Whatsoever is right and proper for me to do in any circumstance, I should do with an eye single to the glory of God, and by so doing I shall be bearing fruit unto Him. The testimony of the little maid who said, "I know I am converted, and my mistress knows I am converted too, because I sweep under the mats now," has gone around the world, and wherever this gospel is preached it is told for a memorial of her. She was right, for even in the most commonplace duties she was bearing fruit for God, and she sought to glorify Him by the faithful performance of her responsibilities, done not with eye-service as a man-pleaser, but as pleasing "God which trieth the heart."

Then we have, "Increasing in the knowledge of God." This is more than the knowledge of the Word of God, though undoubtedly the one leads to the other, for God has made Himself known through His Word. But we increase in the knowledge of God as we walk with Him from day to day, learning more of His love and grace, His tender compassion, His care for those who trust Him; and proving, too, how solemn a thing it is to deviate from the path of obedience and thus be exposed to the rod of correction. We know God as we walk with Him. We walk with Him as we obey His Word.

> We know Him as we could not know
> Through heaven's golden years;
> We there shall see His glorious face,
> On earth they saw His tears;
>
> The touch that heals the broken heart
> Is never felt above;
> His angels know His blessedness,
> His way-worn saints His love.

We shall thank Him for all eternity for every trial along our pilgrim path that gave Him a new opportunity to display His grace and to manifest His heart to us, His needy people, so dependent upon His power and grace.

As we thus go on with Him, we will be strengthened with all might according to His glorious power, and this "unto all patience and long-suffering with joyfulness." How much have we here upon which our souls may well meditate? It is He who supplies strength, giving all needed power in order that we may overcome in every adverse circumstance, according to the might of His glory. What room is there for discouragement as temptations and trials surround me and seem about to overwhelm me, if I realize that the very same spiritual dynamic, that wondrous energy which raised Christ from the dead, operates in me by the Spirit that I may be even more than victorious through Him who loves me!

But we might have supposed that all this manifestation of divine energy would result in producing some great outward display that would astonish and amaze an unbelieving world. But no it is "unto all patience." I need this dynamic force so to keep the flesh in subjection that I can patiently endure whatsoever God in His wisdom sees fit to let me go through while in this wilderness world. Neither will I simply endure with stoic resignation, such as even a pagan philosopher might exhibit, but God would have me patiently wait upon Him and rest in His love even amid circumstances that press hard upon my soul, with long-suffering, that is, uncomplaining endurance. But there is even more than this. In the hour of trial a song of gladness will well up in the heart where the will of God is supreme. And so he adds, "With joyfulness."

Here is something that the natural man knows nothing of—joy in the time of trial; gladness in the time of hardship; songs in the night, though the darkness be overwhelming; praises to the God of my salvation when nature shrinks and trembles. It was thus the martyrs could rejoice in the arena when thrown to the lions, or exult in the Lord when the flames leaped up around them as they suffered at the stake. And myriads of sufferers all through the Christian era have been able to testify to the sustaining grace of God, when the spirit seemed about to be overwhelmed. "The joy of the Lord is your strength."

The three verses that follow are in marked contrast to those we have just been considering. We have now thanksgiving instead of prayer. Here all is positive and eternally settled. The blessings enumerated are ours from the moment we believe in the Lord Jesus Christ and are absolutely nonforfeitable. To pray for these is to dishonor God by casting doubt upon His Word. Notice the three *haths* and the one *have* of the King James Version; words that speak of present possession. Faith lays hold of such testimonies and rejoices in the assurance that these wondrous blessings are to be enjoyed even now.

First we read, "Giving thanks unto the Father, which hath made us meet to be partakers of the inheritance of the saints in light." This is true of every Christian, and there are no degrees in this divine fitness. We are made meet to be partakers of our glorious inheritance the instant we are cleansed from our sins and receive the new nature, which is imparted by a divine operation when we are born of God. How different are the thoughts of even some of the best of men! How often we hear it said of some devoted and aged believer, "He is fit for heaven at last." But he was just as truly fit for heaven the moment he received Christ as he is at the end of a long life of devoted service. Fitness does not depend upon experience. But in this connection it is well to remember that there is something more than the Father's house, the inheritance of the saints in light, before us.

It is important that we should also have in mind the coming glorious kingdom. In 2 Peter 1:10–11 we are told, "Wherefore the rather, brethren, give diligence to make your calling and election sure: for if ye do these things, ye shall never fall: for so an entrance shall be ministered unto you abundantly into the everlasting kingdom of our Lord and Saviour Jesus Christ." The expression, "these things," refers to the various Christian virtues enumerated in verses 5–7. It is through these things we are fitted for a place in the coming kingdom, but it is the justifying, regenerating grace of God that alone makes us meet for our heavenly inheritance. In other words, it is important that we distinguish between salvation by grace and reward for service.

We next read, "Who hath delivered us from the power [or, authority] of darkness, and hath translated us into the kingdom of [the Son of his love]." This is a different kingdom to that of which we have been reading in 2 Peter. It is the present sphere where Christ's authority is owned, the kingdom which we see and enter by new birth. This kingdom consists not of "meat and drink, but [of] righteousness, peace and joy in the Holy Ghost." As born of God we have lost our old standing as sons of fallen Adam in the satanic kingdom of darkness. We have been brought out of the darkness into the marvelous light of children of God, and it is here, of course, that responsibility comes in to walk as children of light. J. N. Darby was once asked, "But suppose a Christian turned his back on the light. What then?" He replied, "Then the light will shine upon his back!" Most blessed it is to see this. We are in the light in all the value of the precious atoning blood of our Lord Jesus Christ sprinkled upon the mercy seat, the very throne of God from which the light shines.

Lastly we read, "In Him we have redemption through His blood, even the forgiveness of sins." There is some question as to the manuscript's authority of the expression, "through His blood." The best editors generally omit it. It seems to have been inserted from Ephesians 1:7. But that does not for a moment touch the truth of which we have been speaking. It would only suggest the fuller character of redemption which is both by blood and by power. The blood having been shed, the omnipotent power of God makes redemption real to the believer, whose sins have all been forgiven and who has been lifted completely out of those circumstances in which he was once exposed to the judgment of God. As the soul meditates on the wonderful truths so succinctly presented in these three verses the heart will surely go out to God in worship and the life be yielded for devoted service!

Let me recapitulate, as I close:

- He hath made us meet for the inheritance of the saints in light.
- He hath delivered us from the authority of darkness.
- He hath translated us into the kingdom of the Son of His love.
- We have redemption through His blood.

Blessed certainties these that tell in unmistakable terms of our eternal security if once in Christ!

CHAPTER 4

CHRIST THE FIRSTBORN: TWOFOLD HEADSHIP OF CHRIST AND TWOFOLD RECONCILIATION

Colossians 1:15–22

Who is the image of the invisible God, the firstborn of every creature: for by him were all things created, that are in heaven, and that are in earth, visible and invisible, whether they be thrones, or dominions, or principalities, or powers: all things were created by him, and for him: and he is before all things, and by him all things consist. And he is the head of the body, the church: who is the beginning, the firstborn from the dead; that in all things he might have the preeminence. For it pleased the Father that in him should all fulness dwell. (vv. 15–19)

We have had our Lord Jesus before us as the Son of God's love in whom we have redemption. Our attention is now directed to Him as the One who has made God known to us. Coming into the world as man He is the image of the invisible God—that God who to the Gnostic could never be known or understood. We are told in John 1:18, "No man hath seen God at any time; the only begotten Son, which is in the bosom of the Father, he hath declared him." Five times in the New Testament He is called the Only Begotten, and this endearing term always refers to what He is from eternity, with no thought of generation connected with it. It implies unity in life and nature. Isaac is called in Hebrews 11:17 Abraham's only begotten son—yet Ishmael was also his son. But the link between Abraham and Isaac was of a unique character. And so, as the Only Begotten, our Lord is the unique Son, eternally that, for if He be not the eternal Son, then we lose the eternal Father too.

God existed from all eternity as three Persons—Father, Son, and Holy Spirit—but never became visible to created eyes whether of angels or men until the Holy Babe was born in Bethlehem. The Son was as truly the invisible God as the Father or the Spirit until the incarnation. Then He was seen of angels, and later on by men. As thus begotten of God of a virgin mother without any human father, He is Son of God in a new sense. And it is as such He is owned of the Father as the firstborn of every creature, or perhaps the expression would be better rendered, the firstborn of all creation. It is not that He is Himself created, but He is the Head of all that has been created.

It will be seen from what has been said above that the title *Firstborn* is not to be taken solely as a divine title, though He is divine who bears this name. But it is as Man He is owned of God the Father as the Firstborn. And how right it is that such a title should be conferred upon Him, for "by him were all things created." Coming into the world as Man, He takes that place in virtue of the dignity of His person. His is the glory of the Firstborn because He is the Creator. The firstborn is the heir and preeminent one. It is important to remember that in Scripture the firstborn is not necessarily the one born first. Many instances might be cited where the one born first was set to one side and the right of the firstborn given to another. One only needs to mention the cases of Ishmael and Isaac, Esau and Jacob, Reuben and Joseph, Manasseh and Ephraim, to which many more might be added. The first man is set aside and the second man is acknowledged as the firstborn. And so Adam and all his race are set to one side as unfit to retain authority over the world in order that Christ, the Second Man, the Lord from heaven, may be acknowledged as the Firstborn.

It will be seen how tremendously all this would weigh against the Gnostic conception of a created Jesus to whom the Christ, a divine emanation, came upon His enlightenment following His baptism, and who left Him again at the cross. It was the eternal Son who stooped in grace to become the Son of God as born of a virgin. It should never be lost sight of that His Sonship is spoken of in these two distinct ways in Scripture. As the Eternal Son, pre-incarnate, He is called "the Son," "the Son of the Father," and also the "Son of God," but the latter term generally refers to what He became when He took humanity into relation with deity and became God and Man in one Person with two natures, in accordance with the word of the angel, addressed to His virgin mother, "That Holy One, who shall be born of thee, shall be called the Son of God." It is necessary to be very accurate in our thinking when considering this great mystery, and not to let our thoughts run beyond Holy Scripture. It was of the virgin-born Savior that Micah prophesied, saying, "But thou, Bethlehem Ephratah, though thou be little among the thousands of Judah, yet out of thee shall he come forth unto me that is to be ruler in Israel; whose goings forth have been from of old, from everlasting," or, as the margin puts it, "from the days of eternity" (Mic. 5:2).

The five passages in which He is called the Only Begotten, if carefully weighed, will make this clear.

> The Word became flesh, and tabernacled among us, (and we beheld his glory, the glory as of the only begotten of the Father), full of grace and truth. (John 1:14, literal rendering)

> No man hath seen God at any time, the only begotten Son, subsisting in the bosom of the Father, he hath told him out. (John 1:18, literal rendering)

> For God so loved the world, that he gave his only begotten Son, that whosoever believeth in him should not perish, but have everlasting life. (John 3:16)

> He that believeth on him is not condemned: but he that believeth not is condemned already, because he hath not believed in the name of the only begotten Son of God. (John 3:18)

> In this was manifested the love of God toward us, because that God sent his only begotten Son into the world, that we might live through him. (1 John 4:9)

The five other passages referred to in which He is called the Firstborn, or First Begotten, are as follows:

For whom he did foreknow, he also did predestinate to be conformed to the image of his Son, that he might be the firstborn among many brethren. (Rom. 8:29)

Who is the image of the invisible God, the firstborn of every creature [or, of all creation]. (Col. 1:15)

And he is the head of the body, the church; who is the beginning, the firstborn from the dead; that in all things he might have the preeminence. (Col. 1:18)

And when he bringeth the firstborn into the habitable earth, again he saith, And let all the angels of God worship him. (Heb. 1:6, literal rendering)

Jesus Christ, who is the faithful witness, and the first begotten of [or, from among] the dead, and the prince of the kings of the earth. (Rev. 1:5)

It was He who brought all things into being. "Without him was not anything made that was made." All the inhabitants of heaven and of earth owe their lives to Him. Beings visible or invisible are all the creatures of His hand. Angels, no matter how great their dignity, whether thrones, or dominions, or principalities, or powers, all were created by Him and for His glory. The Gnostics placed these varied ranks of exalted beings between Him and God, but He is shown to be superior to them all, for He brought them into being. He is Himself the uncreated Son who became Man to accomplish the work of redemption. Higher than all angels, He was made a little lower than they for the suffering of death.

In verse 17 His priority is insisted on in another way. "He is before all things." By the term "all things" we understand all that has been created, whether personal or impersonal. He Himself existed as the eternal Word before them all. "In the beginning was the Word, and the Word was with God, and the Word was God." Full Deity is ascribed to Him, yet distinct personality. Moreover, it is He who sustains the universe, for "by Him all things consist," or, "hold together." It is His hand that holds the stars in their courses, directs the planets in their orbits, and controls the laws of the universe. How great is His dignity, and yet how low did He stoop for our salvation!

But He is firstborn in another sense in verse 18. Man rejected Him saying,

"This is the heir; come, let us kill him, that the inheritance may be ours." So they slew Him, hanging Him on a tree. But it was then that God made His soul an offering for sin, and He accomplished the great work of redemption for which He came. "[He died], the just for the unjust, that he might bring us to God." But having been delivered on account of our offenses, He was raised again on account of our justification. As brought again from the dead He became the Firstborn in a new sense, the Head of the new creation. As Man on earth in incarnation there was no union with Him. Union is in resurrection. He was alone as the Incarnate Son here in the world. As He Himself says: "Except a corn of wheat fall into the ground and die, it abideth alone: but if it die, it shall bring forth much fruit." It is in resurrection that He is hailed as the Firstborn from among the dead. As such He becomes the Head of the body, the church; the Beginning of the creation of God; Firstborn among many brethren; the Resurrection King-Priest; the One who is yet to rule the world in manifested glory; the Melchizedek of the age to come, as Hebrews shows us.

Verse 19 is admittedly difficult to translate euphoniously, and in our English version the words "the Father" have been supplied in order to complete what seems like an incomplete sentence. But it should be carefully noted that there is nothing in the original to answer to the term "the Father." It is rather "the fulness" that was pleased to dwell in Jesus. And if this verse is connected with verse 9 of chapter 2 we shall understand at once what is in view. "In him all the fulness [of the Godhead] was pleased to dwell." Deity has been fully manifested in Jesus our adorable Lord. This is the mystery of godliness of 1 Timothy 3:16. The Gnostics used this term, "the fulness," or *pleroma*, for the divine essence, dwelling in unapproachable light; and in a lesser sense for the illumination that comes when one reaches the higher plane of knowledge. But all the divine *pleroma* dwelt in Jesus. All that God is, He is, so that we may now say, "We know God in knowing him." He has fully manifested Him.

As we ponder the wondrous truths brought before us in these verses the spiritual mind will feel more and more that we have here mysteries of a character beyond the ability of the human mind to grasp. Here is truth for pious meditation, to stir the soul to worship and thanksgiving, not at all for the exercise of the intellect in theological speculations. As we read we would bow our hearts in lowly adoration and thus gaze upon the face of Him who has come forth from the glory that He had with the Father in all the past eternity in order to bring us into the knowledge of God.

In the next section we are told of a twofold reconciliation.

And, having made peace through the blood of his cross, by him to reconcile all things unto himself; by him, I say, whether they be things in earth, or things in heaven. And you, that were sometime alienated and enemies in your mind by wicked works, yet now hath he reconciled in the body of his flesh through death, to present you holy and unblameable and unreproveable in his sight. (vv. 20–22)

In the portion we have just considered, Christ has been presented as the Firstborn in two distinct ways. We have had His twofold Headship: first over all creation and then as Head of the body, the church. In the verses now before us we have reconciliation presented in a double aspect. First, we have the future reconciliation of all things and then present individual reconciliation. He in whom all the fullness dwells has made peace through the blood of His cross. Man is never called upon in Scripture to make his own peace with God. He is viewed as alienated and an enemy, manifestly so, through wicked works.

Sin has come in between God and man, requiring expiation before the guilty rebel could be received by God in peace. Not only on earth, but in heaven has sin lifted up its serpenthead. In fact, it was in heaven that sin began, when Lucifer apostatized, leading with him a vast number of the angelic hosts. Therefore the heavens themselves were unclean in the sight of God and had to be purified by a better sacrifice than those offered under the law. On the cross Christ tasted death, and so far-reaching are the results of His work that eventually all things in earth and in heaven will be reconciled to God upon the basis of what He there accomplished. Whether for the universe or for the individual sinner, He made peace through the blood of His cross. Yet rebels remain in spite of the fact that peace has been made.

We may understand it if we remember that two nations which have been at war with one another may through their plenipotentiaries have agreed on terms of peace, and yet guerilla bands may insist on fighting, ignoring the peace that has been made. So men and demons still persist in refusing to own the divine authority, notwithstanding the fact that,

> Jesus' blood, through earth and skies,
> Mercy, free boundless mercy, cries.

For angels the terms of peace offer no pardon, but to the sinful sons of Adam clemency is extended, and he who will may trust in Christ and thus be reconciled to God. "Being justified by faith, we have peace with God through our Lord Jesus Christ" (Rom. 5:1).

The reconciliation of all things includes two spheres, and two only. The time will come when all in earth and all in heaven will be happily reconciled to God. When it is a question of subjugation, as in Philippians 2:10, there are three spheres. Heavenly, earthly, and infernal beings are at last to own the authority of our Lord Jesus Christ. But there is no hope held out in Scripture that the sad inhabitants of the infernal regions will ever be reconciled to God.

The reconciliation of verse 20 carries us on to the new heaven and the new earth where righteousness will dwell and the tabernacle of God shall be with men, and all the redeemed with the elect angels abide with Him in holy harmony. Sin has ruptured the state of peace and harmony that once existed between God and His creatures. Christ in death has wrought reconciliation, and so made it possible for that lost concord to be reestablished, but in new creation.

This reconciliation is already accomplished for individual sinners who "were sometime alienated and enemies in their mind by wicked works," but who through infinite grace have been reconciled to God by the death of His Son. It is the soul's apprehension by faith of the infinite love of the offended Deity manifested in the death of the cross that destroys the enmity and draws out the affections of the renewed man to God revealed in Christ. Well may the apostle exclaim elsewhere,

> And all things are of God, who hath reconciled us to himself by Jesus Christ, and hath given to us the ministry of reconciliation; to wit, that God was in Christ, reconciling the world unto himself, not imputing their trespasses unto them; and hath committed unto us the word of reconciliation. Now then we are ambassadors for Christ, as though God did beseech you by us: we pray you in Christ's stead, be ye reconciled to God. (2 Cor. 5:18–20)

It is not the holy, wondrous life of Christ that has thus reconciled us. It is His sacrificial death. And as a result of that death we shall eventually be presented before God the Father unblameable in holiness and unreproveable in His sight. The sentence is not concluded in verse 22, but the passage that follows introduces a new subject and therefore must be considered in a different connection.

In leaving the verses which we have been considering, let us bear in mind the great outstanding truths that they would teach us. He who is the image of the invisible God has made peace for us by the blood of His cross. Now in resurrection He is our exalted Head, and we are the members of His body. As Head, He is concerned about every redeemed one here on earth, who has thus, through grace, been united to Him. To own Him as Head is our first responsibility. We are to let nothing put Him at a distance or hinder our loyal subjection to Him through whom we have been reconciled to God.

CHAPTER 5

Paul's Twofold Ministry

Colossians 1:23–29

If ye continue in the faith grounded and settled, and be not moved away from the hope of the gospel, which ye have heard, and which was preached to every creature which is under heaven; whereof I Paul am made a minister; who now rejoice in my sufferings for you, and fill up that which is behind of the afflictions of Christ in my flesh for his body's sake, which is the church: whereof I am made a minister, according to the dispensation of God which is given to me for you, to fulfil the word of God. (vv. 23–25)

The *if* with which verse 23 begins has been the occasion of much perplexity to timid souls who hardly dare to accept the truth of the believer's eternal security, so conscious are they of their own weakness and insufficiency. But, rightly understood, there is nothing here to disturb any sincere believer in the Lord Jesus Christ. There are a number of similar *ifs* in the New Testament, and all with precisely the same object in view—the testing of profession. In 1 Corinthians 15:1–2 we read, "Moreover, brethren, I declare unto you the gospel which I preached unto you, which also ye have received, and wherein ye stand; by which also ye are saved, if ye keep in memory what I preached unto you, unless ye have believed in vain." Here the *if* is inserted in order to exercise the consciences of any who, having professed to believe the gospel, are in danger of forgetting the message, so proving that they have never really received the truth into their hearts. He would have them carefully examine their foundations. Many there are who readily profess to adopt Christianity and unite themselves outwardly with the people of God, who have never truly turned to the Lord in repentance and rested their souls upon His finished work. Such endure for a time but soon forget the claims of the gospel when satanic allurements would draw them away.

In Hebrews 3:6 we have another such *if.* "But Christ as a son over his own house; whose house are we, if we hold fast the confidence and the rejoicing of the hope firm unto the end." The meaning is plain. It is not enough to profess to have the Christian hope. Those who are real will hold fast unto the end, as we also read in 10:38–39 of the same epistle. Endurance is the proof of reality. What God implants in the soul is lasting, and we may be assured that He who hath begun a good work in any one will perform it until the day of Jesus Christ, the time when He shall come for His ransomed people to complete in glory what His grace began on earth.

Paul did not pretend to say who of the Colossians were really born of God. While he had confidence that most of them were, he wrote in such a way as to stir up the consciences of any who were becoming slack. A readiness to adopt new and fanciful systems was a cause for grave concern. Those who are really children of God, grounded and strengthened in the truth, are not of the number who will be moved away from the hope of the gospel. They know too well what it has already done for them to lightly turn away from it to some new and untried theory.

This gospel they had heard, as in the providence of God it had been preached in all the creation under heaven. This is probably a better translation than that of the King James Version. It is hardly thinkable that the apostle meant that every creature in the habitable earth had heard the gospel. But it is a wonderful testimony to the devotion of the early believers that even within one generation after our Lord's ascension the evangel had been carried throughout the known world. Of this gospel Paul was made "minister." The indefinite article does not really help. It only lends color to the idea which came in later, that the ministry is a special class to which all believers do not belong. The apostle is not claiming that he is a minister in the sense in which that term has been used in later years. He was one addicted to the work of the ministry. That is, the gospel had been committed to him by God whom he served, as he says elsewhere, with his spirit in the gospel of God's Son. This gospel ministry has been committed to all believers, and Paul is a sharer with others in making the testimony known. But in a preeminent way it was given to him to reveal it. As preached by Paul, it bears the distinctive character of "the gospel of the glory."

Another ministry had also been given to him, even that of the assembly, the body of Christ. So he goes on to say that he rejoices in whatsoever he might be called upon to suffer on behalf of the people of God, as in doing this he was filling up what was lacking of the afflictions of Christ in his own flesh. That is true of every real servant of God. To such a one the people of the Lord will ever be precious. And he will realize that in serving them and enduring trial on their behalf he is ministering in place of his absent Lord. Christ suffered once for all on the cross to put away sin. His faithful servants suffer in fellowship with Him for the perfecting of the saints, "for His body's sake, which is the church." The more devoted one is to Christ's interests down here, during His absence in heaven, the more one will enter into this phase of suffering. It is godly shepherd care that he has in mind, enduring affliction for the blessing of Christ's beautiful flock.

Of the church Paul was made minister according to the dispensation of God given to him on our behalf to complete the divine testimony or to fill up the Word of God. The whole counsel of God was not made known until Paul received this revelation of the mystery. This dispensation, or stewardship (for the two words are exactly the same in Greek), he unfolds more fully elsewhere, noticeably in the epistle to the Ephesians, which, as previously intimated, is the correlative to that to the Colossians. It was a special revelation given not to the Twelve, but to him as the apostle of the new dispensation. He goes on with this theme in the verses that follow.

> Even the mystery which hath been hid from ages and from generations, but now is made manifest to his saints: to whom God would make known what is the riches of the glory of this mystery among the Gentiles; which is Christ in you, the hope of glory: whom we preach, warning every man, and teaching every man in all wisdom; that we may present every man perfect in Christ Jesus: whereunto I also labour, striving according to his working, which worketh in me mightily. (vv. 26–29)

It is important to remember that the mysteries of the New Testament are not necessarily things mysterious or abstruse. They are rather sacred secrets made known to the initiated.[1]

These divine secrets could never have been discovered by human reason, nor even by the child of God unless a special revelation had been given. The Gnostics made much of the mysteries of their systems. The Christian mysteries are in vivid contrast to these dreams of insubject men.

The mystery of the church as the body of Christ was never made known in Old Testament times, nor yet in the days when our Lord was on the earth. We are told distinctly it had been "hid from ages and from generations, but now is made manifest to the saints." The divine method of making it known was by a special revelation to the apostle Paul, as he tells us in Ephesians 3. But this revelation was not for him only. It was a ministry committed to him to pass on to the saints, "To whom God did make known the wealth of the splendor of this sacred secret among the nations, which is Christ among the Gentiles, the hope of glory" (author's translation). The Old Testament Scripture clearly predicted the calling of the Gentiles, but always in subjection to Israel. During the present dispensation Israel, as we read in Romans 11, is set aside because of unbelief, and Christ is working among the nations, attracting weary hearts to Himself altogether apart from any thought of Jewish priority. Believing Jews and Gentiles are united by the Holy Spirit's baptism into the one body, and thus all fleshly distinctions are done away. The middle wall of partition is broken down. *This* is the mystery.

Christ Himself, the Head of this body, is the apostle's theme. Note his words, "whom we preach." To substitute *what* for *whom* we preach is a serious mistake. Christianity is centered in a Person, and no one preaches the gospel who does not preach Christ. When there is faith in Him the Spirit unites the believer to Him.

How earnest was the apostle in seeking to lead Christians into the knowledge of this precious truth, "warning every man, and teaching every man in all wisdom." His was the true pastor's heart, and he combined in a marvelous way the teacher's gift with this. The subject of his ministry was the perfecting of the saints, as he says elsewhere. He would present every man complete or full grown in Christ Jesus. To this end he earnestly labored according to that divine energy which wrought so powerfully in him for the salvation of souls and the upbuilding of the people of God.

False teachers would turn the eyes of the saints away from Christ, the glorified Head of the body, in order that they might occupy them with specious systems of satanic origin, and thus draw away disciples after themselves, as Paul had warned the Ephesian elders. But all true Spirit-given ministry is Christocentric. Every faithful minister of the new dispensation would lift up the Lord Jesus before the admiring gaze of His people so that, occupied with Him, they might be transfigured into His likeness. Like John the Baptist he will say, "He must increase, but I must decrease."

No man really preaches the whole truth today who does not enter into the twofold ministry of this section of Colossians—the gospel and the church. The former is proclaimed to sinners and is the power of God unto salvation to every one who believes. The latter is taught to saints and builds them up in the faith as to their present privileges, and corresponding responsibilities. I am called upon, not only to win sinners to Christ that they may be saved from impending wrath, but I am to seek to make "good churchmen" out of those already saved. This is not to insist on what is called denominational loyalty, nor to endeavor to sectionalize the saints and bring them into bondage to legal principles and practices for which there is no biblical warrant. But it is to show them their position as in the new creation, linked with their risen, glorified Head, and to lead them into the recognition of the unity of the body, in which all believers have a part. Thus they may endeavor to keep the unity formed by the Holy Spirit, as they walk together in the uniting bond of peace.

Sad indeed is it when this very truth becomes a means of dividing those of like precious faith when perverted by men of sectarian spirit and narrow, cramped sympathies who are more concerned about building up local "causes" than edifying the body of Christ!

That saints are not to neglect local responsibilities, out of which grows the relationship of church to church, is perfectly true. But it is not a unity or confederacy of assemblies that is denominated "the unity of the Spirit." It is rather that abiding unity which the Holy Spirit has formed by baptizing believers into one body. If I set at nought any fellow believer I am to that extent failing to keep this unity. As members one of another, having the same care one for the other, we show in a practical way the truth that we are one in Christ.

CHAPTER 6

CHRIST THE TRUE WISDOM: THE REVELATION OF THE MYSTERY OF GOD

Colossians 2:1–7

For I would that ye knew what great conflict I have for you, and for them at Laodicea, and for as many as have not seen my face in the flesh; that their hearts might be comforted, being knit together in love, and unto all riches of the full assurance of understanding, to the acknowledgement of the mystery of God, and of the Father, and of Christ; in whom are hid all the treasures of wisdom and knowledge. And this I say, lest any man should beguile you with enticing words. For though I be absent in the flesh, yet am I with you in the spirit, joying and beholding your order, and the stedfastness of your faith in Christ. As ye have therefore received Christ Jesus the Lord, so walk ye in him: rooted and built up in him, and stablished in the faith, as ye have been taught, abounding therein with thanksgiving. (vv. 1–7)

Men who know little of the deep convictions that stirred the heart of the apostle Paul will have difficulty in realizing the intensity of his feelings when the truth of God was called in question, and the people of the Lord were in danger of being corrupted by false doctrine and turned aside from the simplicity that is in Christ. He says, "For I would have you know what intense agony I have for you." He was not one who could play fast and loose with revealed truth. His very soul was tortured when Christ was dishonored by those who professed His name. He was not a self-complacent liberal in theology carelessly tolerant of any teaching, no matter how pernicious, so long as outward unity is maintained. To know that both at Colosse and Laodicea designing men were seeking to seduce the saints from their first love, who was Christ Himself, caused him intense concern. That the enemy was largely successful at Laodicea we know, for John, as the amanuensis of the glorified Son of Man, writing to them later from Patmos, charges them with being neither cold nor hot. Proud of their culture and wealth they were indifferent to Christ. It is from this Paul sought to save them, and it is to be hoped he succeeded at Colosse.

The truth unites. Error divides. He desires "that their hearts might be comforted, being knit together in love, and unto all riches of the full assurance of understanding, to the acknowledgement of the mystery of God, . . . [even] Christ" (v. 2). There is some manuscript diversity in regard to the last part of this sentence. The King James Version reads, "The mystery of God, and of the Father, and of Christ," which is admittedly peculiar. One could understand, "The mystery of God, even of the Father, and of Christ," and it might be so translated. But the reading of some manuscripts, "The mystery of God, even Christ," seems clearer and is probably correct.

It is the great divine mystery of the new man, as we read in 1 Corinthians 12:12–13: "For as the body is one, and hath many members, and all the members of that one body, being many, are one body: so also is Christ. For by one Spirit are we all baptized into one body, whether we be Jews or Gentiles, whether we be bond or free; and have been all made to drink into one Spirit." The definite article before "Christ" does not appear in the King James Version, but probably should be there. It is the mystical Christ that is in view, and I take it that we have a similar idea in Colossians 2:2. The mystery of God is that which He has now revealed regarding Christ as Head of the body, and consequently of the entire new creation. As believers enter into the truth of this they are delivered not only from vain speculations but from fleshly strivings, for all perfection is found in Christ. So the apostle would have them understand the wealth of this great mystery as they enjoy the full assurance of understanding in order to its acknowledgment. In Hebrews 6:11 we read of the full assurance of hope, and in 10:22 of the same epistle we get the full assurance of faith. These together establish the soul and set it free from doubt and fear.

In Christ, or if you prefer, in this mystery of God now revealed, are hid all the treasures of wisdom and knowledge. It is not necessary to go elsewhere, investigating human systems and philosophies, for an explanation of the mystery of the universe and the relations of the Creator to His creatures. All these are fully told out in Christ. As we learn to know Him better and apprehend the truth concerning Him, every question is answered, every perplexity made clear, and every doubt dissolved. Why turn aside to idle speculations, no matter how pretentious, when God has spoken in His Son and given His Holy Word to lead us by the Spirit into all truth? Paul says all this in order to protect the saints from being led astray by persuasive talk or with enticing words. Advocates of error delight to clothe their evil systems in most attractive phraseology, to entrap the souls of the unwary. Only the truth of God can preserve from such. It is important to remember that no amount of intellectual culture or human learning can take the place of divine revelation. If God has not spoken we may speculate and reason as we please. But if He has given the truth in His Word there is an end to all our theorizings.

In this chapter he shows us how Christ is the antidote for human philosophy, Jewish legality, Oriental mysticism, and carnal asceticism. These have no place in Christianity. Christ supersedes them all. And Paul knew through the testimony of Epaphras what Christ had meant to these Colossian saints from the time of their conversion, and he was very jealous lest they should now be turned aside. Though not with them in the flesh, he was one with them in spirit, and rejoiced in all he had heard of their godly order and their steadfast confidence in Christ. This was how they began; moreover, they had continued in the same paths and he would have them continue so. Having received Christ Jesus the Lord, that is, having trusted Him as Savior and owned Him as Master, he would now have them walk in Him, not turning aside to any new system or perversion of the truth. He desired to see them rooted and built up in Him—rooted like a tree, sending its roots deep down into the soil. He would have all their hidden sources of supply so centered in Christ. Built up like a building founded on a rock and firmly established, he would so have them recognize Christ as their only foundation.

He uses the same double figure in Ephesians 3:17, "That Christ may dwell in your hearts by faith; that ye, being rooted and grounded in love." God is love, and God has been revealed in Christ. So to be rooted and established in love is to be rooted in and founded upon God, and it is God revealed in Christ. Why then should any go after speculative theories that cannot give the soul peace and which make light of Christ the Head? As thus walking in Him the man would be established in the faith, in accordance with the instruction already received, "abounding therein with thanksgiving." Nothing so causes the soul to overflow with worship and gratitude to God as a deep knowledge of Christ. It is noteworthy that true joy is only found in acquaintance with Him.

It is hardly necessary to make the application to present-day systems. Each one who really knows Christ will readily do that for himself or herself. An illustration may help to make clear what I believe the apostle is here indicating. A follower of Mrs. Eddy, the now-deceased head of the so-called Christian Science cult, labored long to unfold the professed benefits and beauties of that system to a simple Christian woman who, after listening for several hours, found herself utterly unable to follow the specious sophistries and vapid theorizings of her visitor. Finally she exclaimed, "I do not understand what you are getting at. Can you not put it all in simpler terms so that I may know what it is you want me to believe?" "Well," replied the other, "in the first place you must get hold of this: God is principle not a person. You see, my dear, we worship a principle—" "Enough!" exclaimed the other with a relieved expression on her countenance. "That would never do for me! I worship a personal God revealed in Christ, my blessed, adorable Savior." And at once her soul was delivered from the net spread before her by the soft-voiced emissary of Satan who had been endeavoring to ensnare her. And this is ever the test. Every system that makes light of Christ or His atoning blood is from the pit and to be shunned as a viper by all who know Him.

John Newton has well written:

"What think ye of Christ?" is the test,
    To try both your state and your scheme;
You cannot be right in the rest,
    Unless you think rightly of Him:
As Jesus appears in your view—
    As He is beloved or not,
So God is disposed to you,
    And mercy or wrath is your lot.

Some take Him a creature to be—
    A man, or an angel at most;

But they have not feelings like me,
    Nor know themselves wretched and lost.
So guilty, so helpless am I,
    I durst not confide in His blood,
Nor on His protection rely,
    Unless I were sure He is God.

Some call Him a Saviour, in word,
    But mix their own works with His plan;
And hope He His help will afford,
    When they have done all that they can:
If doings prove rather too light
    (A little they own they may fail),
They purpose to make up full weight,
    By casting His name in the scale.

Some style Him "the Pearl of great price,"
    And say, He's the fountain of joys;
Yet feed upon folly and vice,
    And cleave to the world and its toys.
Like Judas, the Saviour they kiss,
    And while they salute Him, betray:
Oh! what will profession like this
    Avail in His terrible day?

If asked what of Jesus I think,
    Though still my best thoughts are but poor,
I say, He's my meat and my drink,
    My life, and my strength, and my store;
My Shepherd, my trust, and my Friend,
    My Saviour from sin and from thrall;
My Hope from beginning to end,
    My Portion, my Lord and my All.

The natural man cannot understand why Christians should insist upon a clear-cut confession of the truth as to Christ. What matters it, he will ask, whether Jesus be a mere man, spiritual beyond most, or be in very deed the Divine Eternal Son become flesh? If a man only, He is still the great Exemplar and the Master-Teacher.

If more than man He is but the manifestation of the Father, and by His life of love and purity has shown us God's attitude toward all mankind and so leads us into a better understanding of God and our relationship to Him.

But this is not the truth of Holy Scripture concerning Him. His holy life—whether He be only human or divinely human—can never put away our sins or fit us to stand uncondemned before the eternal throne. He had to be both God and Man in order that He might make atonement for sin, meeting as Man—yet Man in all perfection—every claim that the throne of outraged Deity had against man. Touch the Person of Christ and you touch His work. If that work was not divinely perfect there remains no other sacrifice for sins and so we are left without a Savior.

But, blessed be God, He who came forth from the Father has glorified Him on the earth, and having finished the work given Him to do has gone back to that glory that He had with the Father before the world was. There He sits, the exalted Man who made purification for sins, on the right hand of the Majesty in the heavens, ever living to make intercession for those His grace has saved. Happy in this knowledge we may well sing, with chastened joy,

> Head of the church! Thou sittest there,
> Thy members all the blessings share—
>   Thy blessing, Lord, is ours:
> Our life Thou art—Thy grace sustains,
> Thy strength in us each vict'ry gains
>   O'er sin and Satan's pow'rs.

May we prove our loyalty to Him, not only by confessing a true Christ with our lips, but by giving Him the supreme place in our lives!

CHAPTER 7

Christ the Antidote to Human Philosophy

Colossians 2:8–10

Beware lest any man spoil you through philosophy and vain deceit, after the tradition of men, after the rudiments of the world, and not after Christ. For in him dwelleth all the fulness of the Godhead bodily. And ye are complete in him, which is the head of all principality and power. (vv. 8–10)

Scripture nowhere condemns the acquisition of knowledge. It is the wisdom of this world, not its knowledge, that is foolishness with God. Philosophy is but worldly wisdom. It is the effort of the human mind to solve the mystery of the universe. It is not an exact science, for the philosophers have never been able to come to any satisfactory conclusion as to either the "why" or the "wherefore" of things. "The Greeks seek after wisdom," we are told, and it was they who led the way for all future generations in philosophical theorizing. Before a divine revelation came it was quite natural and proper that man should seek by wisdom to solve the riddles that nature was constantly propounding. But now that God has spoken this is no longer necessary, and it may become grave infidelity. From Plato

147

to Kant, and from Kant to the last of the moderns, one system has overturned another, so that the history of philosophy is a story of contradictory, discarded hypotheses. This is not to say that the philosophers were or are dishonest men, but it is to say that many of them have failed to avail themselves of that which would unravel every knot and solve every problem, namely, the revelation of God in Christ as given in the Holy Scriptures.

Plato yearned for a divine Word—*logos*—which would come with authority and make everything plain. That Word is *Christ* of whom John writes, "In the beginning was the Word, and the Word was with God, and the Word was God." And again, "The Word became flesh, and tabernacled among us, and we beheld His glory, the glory as of the only begotten of the Father, full of grace and truth" (author's translation). The Word is no longer hidden. We do not need to search for it. "The word is nigh thee, even in thy mouth, and in thy heart: . . . that if thou shalt confess with thy mouth the Lord Jesus, and shalt believe in thine heart that God hath raised him from the dead, thou shalt be saved." Socrates pondering the, to him, unsolvable problems relating to possible future rewards and punishments, said, "It may be, Plato, that the Deity can forgive sins, but I do not see how." No such perplexities need trouble any honest mind now, for what philosophy could not explain, the gospel has made clear, that gospel in which is revealed the righteousness of God for sinful men. Apart from this divine revelation the wisest philosopher of the twentieth century knows no more in regard to the origin and destiny of man than the Attic philosophers of so long ago.

Two great systems were still contending for the mastery over the minds of men in the Western world when Paul wrote this letter to the Colossians—Stoicism and Epicureanism. The one said: Live nobly and death cannot matter. Hold appetite in check. Become indifferent to changing conditions. Be not uplifted by good fortune nor cast down by adversity. The man is more than circumstances, the soul is greater than the universe. Epicureanism said: All is uncertain. We know not whence we came. We know not whither we go. We only know that after a brief life we disappear from this scene, and it is vain to deny ourselves any present joy in view of possible future ill. "Let us eat and drink, for tomorrow we die." To many of the former class the Christian message appealed, and one has only to read 1 Corinthians 9:24–27 or Philippians 4:11–13 to see how readily Paul's message would lay hold of an honest Stoic. With Epicureanism, Christianity had nothing in common. But while the Stoic might find in Christianity the fulfillment of his heart's yearning, there was not in his philosophy anything the Christian needed, for everything that was best in that system he already had in Christ.

Besides these two great outstanding philosophical schools there were many lesser systems among both the Greeks and Romans, all of them seeking to draw away disciples to themselves. The Gnostics embodied parts of all the different schools of thought in their new system. From the weird guesses embodied in the Pythagorean fables down to the evolutionary theories of the present time, the church of God is still in conflict with these vagrant philosophies.

Against all such the Christian is warned. "Beware lest any man spoil you [i.e., lest any make a prey of you] through philosophy and vain deceit." These may make a great show of learning, and their adherents may look down with contempt from their heights of fancied superiority upon people simple enough to believe the gospel and to accept the Holy Scriptures as the inspired Word of the living God. But with all their pretentiousness they are simply the traditions of man, the rudiments or elements of the world. The apostle thus expresses his contempt for mere reasoning in comparison with divine revelation. These systems that claim so much were after all but elementary. It was the *ABC* of the world offered to those who were in the school of Christ and had left the kindergarten of human tradition far behind. "Can a man by searching find out God?" Impossible. But God is already known in His Son.

It is most important that Christians should see this, particularly the young men who are called of God to be ministers of His Word. It is a sad commentary on conditions in Christendom that in the average theological seminary far more time is given to the study of philosophy than to searching the Scriptures. A minister of an orthodox church said recently, "I could have graduated with honors from my seminary without ever opening the English Bible." Thank God, this is not true of all such training schools, but it is true of perhaps the majority. The result is we have today thousands of professed ministers of Christ, many of them unconverted, and others who, though children of God, have been so stunted and hindered by their philosophical education that they are utterly unable to open up the Scriptures to others, for they are so ignorant of the Word themselves. Christianity owes no debt to Greek, Roman, Medieval, or Modern philosophy. It is like the Bible itself in this—

> A glory gilds the sacred page;
> Majestic, like the sun,
> It sheds a light on every age,
> It gives, but borrows none.

A man can be a well-furnished minister of Jesus Christ who has never heard the names of the great philosophers, whether pagan or Christian, and who is utterly ignorant of their systems and hypotheses, providing he will "study to show [himself] approved unto God, a workman that needeth not to be ashamed, rightly dividing the word of truth" (2 Tim. 2:15). The truest culture, intellectual or spiritual, is that which is drawn from the constant study of the Bible. How often as one comes in contact with men of most gracious personality, gentlemanly appearance, high spirituality, and well-trained intellect he finds upon inquiry that they are like John Wesley, "men of one book," and in some instances, hardly conversant with the literature of earth. And in saying this I do not mean to put a premium on ignorance, for as mentioned in the beginning of this address, the knowledge of this world is not under the ban.

The Christian may well avail himself of any legitimate means of becoming better acquainted with the great facts of history, the findings of science, and the beauties of general literature. But let him never put human philosophy in the place of divine revelation. If he studies it at all, and there is no reason why he should not do so, let him begin with this—God has spoken in His Son and in the Holy Scripture He has given us the last words upon every question that philosophy raises. Browning was right when he wrote:

> I say, the acknowledgment of God in Christ,
> Accepted by the reason, solves for thee
> All questions in the earth and out of it,
> And has so far advanced thee to be wise.

When the Savior revealed Himself to the Samaritan woman she found her every question answered as she gazed upon His face.

"In him dwelleth all the fulness of the Godhead bodily." We have already seen in a previous lecture that this word *pleroma*, "fullness," was a favorite term of the Gnostics. It represented to them the sum of the qualities of Deity, and with them Christ was but one of many stepping-stones or intermediaries leading up to the *pleroma*. But here we learn that not only are all the attributes of God seen in Christ, as Arius afterward thought and as Theistic philosophers everywhere admit, but the very essence of the nature of God in all its entirety dwells in Him.

All that God is, is fully told out in Christ. He could say, "He that hath seen me hath seen the Father." So that we may say without hesitation, if any ask as to the character of God, that God is exactly like Jesus. Jesus is the Christ, and in Christ all the fullness of Deity dwells in a body, so that when at last we come into the presence of the Father we shall find in Him one known and loved before, not a stranger still unknown and possibly unknowable. J. N. Darby was thinking of this when he wrote:

> There no stranger-God shall meet thee!
> Stranger thou in courts above:
> He who to His rest shall greet thee,
> Greets thee with a well known love.

"Confessedly great is the mystery of piety, He who hath been manifested in flesh, justified in the Spirit, seen of angels, proclaimed unto the Gentiles, believed on in the world, received up into glory" (1 Tim. 3:16). God is revealed, He is no longer hidden. All His glory shines in the face of Christ Jesus. This solves at once for me as a believer the mystery of the universe.

> And that which seemed to me before
> One wild, confused Babel,
> Is now a fire-tongued Pentecost
> Proclaiming Christ is able;
> And all creation its evangel
> Utters forth abroad
> Into mine ears since once I know
> My Saviour Christ is God.

In verse 10 we are told, "And ye are complete in him, which is the head of all principality and power." The word *complete* is literally "filled full." In Christ dwells all the *pleroma* of Deity, and we have our *pleroma* in Him. We do not need to go elsewhere for illumination or information. "And of his fulness have all we received, and grace for grace. For the law was given by Moses, but grace and truth came by Jesus Christ. No man hath seen God at any time; the only begotten Son, which is in the bosom of the Father, he hath declared him" (John 1:16–18). This revelation floods our being with rapture, fills our cup of joy, and satisfies every demand of the intellect. We are filled full in Him. I would suggest that it is not the believers' standing exactly that is in view here. We have that in Ephesians 1:6. There we are told we are "accepted in the beloved." In that sense we may be said, of course, to be complete in Him, but Colossians 2:10 is rather our state. It is the state of those who have found every need met in Christ, who is the Head of all principality and power.

It has already been pointed out that "principalities" and "powers" are terms relating to different ranks of spiritual beings. In a pretended knowledge of the nature and office of these glorious intelligences, the Gnostics reveled and placed them high above Christ Himself who was, according to them, but one who introduced the initiate into the fellowship of this great serried host leading on up to the invisible God. But the truth is the very opposite, for all the principalities and powers (and these may be good or evil, fallen or unfallen) were created by Him and for Him in whom all the fullness dwells, and He is the Head of all angelic companies as well as human beings.

> No place too high for Him is found,
> No place too high in heaven.

God would have His people ever realize that He who stooped to the depths of shame and suffering of the cross for their salvation is as to the mystery of His wondrous Person, God over all, blessed forever.

It will be observed that verse 10 does not complete the sentence, which is carried right on in verses 11–12. But as what follows is intimately linked with the next subject for our consideration, I leave them now to take them up in the next address, only observing that it is immediately after the declaration of Christ's Headship over all angels that we are told of the depths of His humiliation. For God would never separate the Person and work of our Lord Jesus Christ. But He would have us remember that it was because of His transcendent character and His true Deity that He could undertake the work of purging our sins when He gave Himself a sacrifice on our behalf. He had to be who He was in order to do what He did.

The settlement of the sin question could never be effected by a created being. The issues were too great. Of all men it is written, "None of them can by any means redeem his brother or give to God a ransom for him, for the redemption of the soul costs too much. Therefore, let it alone for ever." This is a somewhat free translation, but authorized by the best Hebrew scholars. It emphasizes what is here brought before us. Low thoughts of Christ result from low thoughts of sin. When I realize the enormity of my iniquity I know that only the Daysman for whom Job yearned can save me from such a load of guilt. He, because He is God and Man, can "lay his hand upon us both," and thus by making atonement for sin bring God and man together in holy, happy harmony.

> . . . Can a mere man do this?
> Yet Christ saith, this He lived and died to do.

Call Christ, then, the illimitable God,
 Or lost!
                                        —Browning

And so we may conclude with this tremendous truth: God has no other answer to all the questionings of the mind of man as to spiritual verities than Christ, and no other is needed, for Christ is the answer to them all. He who refuses Christ refuses God's last word to mankind. He has said everything He has to say in sending Him into the world as the Giver of life and the propitiation for our sins. To turn from Him is to refuse the living incarnation of the Truth and to shut oneself up to error and delusion.

CHAPTER 8

Christ the Antidote to Jewish Legality

Colossians 2:11–17

In whom also ye are circumcised with the circumcision made without hands, in putting off the body of the sins of the flesh by the circumcision of Christ: buried with him in baptism, wherein also ye are risen with him through the faith of the operation of God, who hath raised him from the dead. And you, being dead in your sins and the uncircumcision of your flesh, hath he quickened together with him, having forgiven you all trespasses; blotting out the handwriting of ordinances that was against us, which was contrary to us, and took it out of the way, nailing it to his cross; and having spoiled principalities and powers, he made a show of them openly, triumphing over them in it. Let no man therefore judge you in meat, or in drink, or in respect of an holyday, or of the new moon, or of the sabbath days: which are a shadow of things to come; but the body is of Christ. (vv. 11–17)

This somewhat lengthy section, beginning (as previously mentioned) in the middle of a sentence, might be more easily expounded if divided into two parts, but it is so intimately linked together that I am taking it up as a whole. Philosophy, as we have observed, is the working of the human mind independently of divine revelation. Legality is the endeavor to use a divinely given code, to which may be added precepts of men, as a means either of salvation in the first instance or of growth in grace afterward. Neither of these conceptions is in accordance with Scripture. "By the works of the law there shall no flesh be justified in his sight." This forever bars out legal works as a procuring cause of salvation. "Ye are not under law but under grace." This, as effectually, forbids the thought that holiness of life for the Christian is found in subjecting himself to legal principles. "The strength of sin is the law," we are told in 1 Corinthians 15:56. It is not, as multitudes have supposed, the strength of holiness or the power for righteousness. It is the indwelling Holy Spirit, who occupies us with Christ crucified, raised, and glorified, that is the dynamic of spirituality.

Gnosticism was as much indebted to Judaism, which it perverted to its own ends, and to a weird Jewish Kabalism, as it was to the vapid reasonings of Gentile philosophers and, as we shall see later, to Mithraic and Zoroastrian mysticism. Here the apostle specifically deals with Jewish legality, and shows how Christians have been forever delivered from the law and the legal principle in its entirety, but are now linked with the risen Christ. For the believer to go back to the law for his perfecting in holiness is, as he shows in the epistle to the Galatians, to fall from grace. That is, it is the virtual setting aside of the gospel of grace, forgetting that having begun in the Spirit we are not to be made perfect by the flesh.

There were those ever dogging the footsteps of the great apostle to the Gentiles who sought to pervert his converts by teaching them, "Except ye be circumcised and keep the law of Moses, ye cannot be saved." While the council at Jerusalem gave forth no uncertain sound in opposition to this, it is evident that its decisions were by no means everywhere accepted. It was hard for converts from Judaism to realize their complete deliverance both from the law of Moses as a rule of life, and from the ceremonies and ritual of that law as a means of growth in grace. Here the question at issue is handled in a remarkable manner through the inspiration of the Holy Spirit.

Having declared that we have our completeness in Christ, our exalted Head, he continues: "In whom also ye are circumcised with the circumcision made without hands, in putting off the body . . . of the flesh by the circumcision of Christ." I omit the words "of the sins" as being without sufficient manuscript authority. It is not merely a question of sins here, but the flesh itself that is in view. Circumcision was the cutting off of the flesh physically, and it was given by God to picture the judgment of the carnal nature and its complete setting aside. This is what God has done in the cross of Christ. In His cutting off by death when He stood vicariously in our place, we see the end of the flesh as viewed from the divine standpoint. It is cut off, put to one side, as absolutely worthless. "The flesh," we read, "profiteth nothing." "It is not subject to the law of God, neither indeed can be." Therefore God is making no attempt to improve it. Consequently, there is no place for merit so far as man is concerned. He has none, and, blessed be God, he needs none. All merit is in Another!

The same truth is set forth in Christian baptism. Personally, I have no sympathy with those who in our day would seek to do away altogether with water baptism on the plea that there is now, since the full truth of the church is revealed, only one baptism, and that the baptism of the Holy Spirit. Ephesians 4:4–6 was just as true from Pentecost to Acts 28 as it has ever been since. Paul did not receive the revelation of the mystery after he went to prison. The rapture, which is part of that great mystery, is taught in his earliest epistle—1 Thessalonians. In his postscript to the Roman letter he tells how he has been making known the mystery throughout his ministry, "Made known to all nations for the obedience of faith." To the Ephesian elders he said (as recorded in Acts 20) that he had "not shunned to declare unto [them] the whole counsel of God." That counsel in its entirety had already been made known to him and was proclaimed among the Gentiles. The baptism of the Holy Spirit whereby believers were brought into the body of Christ took place on the day of Pentecost. It was thus that the body, the church, was formed.

There is no hint of any such supernatural work in a widespread manner after Paul's imprisonment. The body had been formed for years, and each believer was added to it when he received the Spirit. The one baptism of Ephesians 4:5, in my judgment, cannot refer to this event because this is already mentioned in the previous verse. In verse 4 we read, "There is one body, and one Spirit, . . . [and] one hope of your calling." This is the full revelation of the mystery, the body formed by the Spirit's baptism, waiting for the coming of the Lord. In verse 5 we have "one Lord, one faith, one baptism." This is responsibility here on earth—Christ owned as Lord, the church called upon to contend for the faith once for all delivered to the saints, and water baptism in the name of the Father, Son, and Holy Spirit in recognition of our subjection to the one Lord. It is not a question of form, formula, or subjects. It is simply the broad fact declared, that Christianity knows only one baptism, and that, of course, is baptism unto the death of Jesus Christ. To speak of the Holy Spirit's baptism as a burial with Christ unto death is nonsense. It is after my identification by faith in death, burial, and resurrection that the Holy Spirit baptizes me into the body.

Nor is this to say that persons who for various reasons, valid or otherwise, may not have been scripturally baptized are not in Christ. In drawing an illustration from what is scripturally correct one does not un-Christianize those who fall short either because of ignorance or willfulness. The argument of verse 12, as I see it, is this: the Christian confesses his identification with a rejected Christ in his baptism. He has owned that the man after the flesh deserved to die. He has died in Christ's death. This, therefore, is the end of the responsible man before God. Necessarily then, it is the end of all self-effort, of every attempt to improve the flesh by subjecting it to ordinances, that is, regulations, whether divinely given as in the Old Testament or humanly devised as in so many unscriptural systems. God is not attempting to improve the old man, He has judged him as too evil for any improvement and has, therefore, set him to one side in death. Baptism is the recognition of this. It is burial unto death.

Some translators read, "Wherein also ye are risen with him," but the preponderance of evidence is, I believe, in favor of the reading, "In whom also ye are risen with him through the faith of the operation of God who hath raised him from the dead." It is through faith in the risen Christ that we become the recipients of the new life and are, henceforth, accounted by God as those who, having gone down into death with Him, are now one with Him in resurrection. What place does legality have here? None whatsoever. To put the new man, the man in Christ, under rules and regulations is contrary to the entire principle of new creation.

This is further emphasized in verse 13. We who once were dead in our trespasses and as Gentiles in the uncircumcision of our flesh have now been made to live together with Him, God having forgiven us all trespasses. The word is the same in each case, and if translated "sins" in the first part of the verse should be "sins" in the last, otherwise "trespasses" in each instance. Moreover, the bond that was against us ("the handwriting," a term which could only be properly used of the Ten Commandments, which we are distinctly told were the handwriting of God, embraced in ten ordinances, or divinely given rules) because of the sinfulness of our natures, making our disobedience to the law, when once it came to our knowledge, a foregone conclusion, and which therefore made it to us a ministration of death and condemnation, has now been taken out of the way and no longer hangs over us as an unfulfilled obligation. Christ nailed it to His cross.

What are we to understand by this expression, "Nailing it to his cross"? It may help us if we remember that it was customary under Roman law when criminals were executed by crucifixion, hanging, or impalement to write out a copy of the law they had broken, or to indicate the nature of their offense on a placard and nail it above the victim's head that all might know how Rome executed vengeance upon those who violated her criminal code. Pilate wrote out the inscription to be placed over the head of Christ Jesus, and that in three languages, Hebrew, Greek, and Latin, that all might know why the patient Sufferer from Galilee was being publicly executed. "This is Jesus of Nazareth, the King of the Jews." As the people read this they understood that he was being crucified because He made Himself a king and was thus disloyal to Caesar.

But as God looked upon that cross His holy eye saw, as it were, another inscription altogether. Nailed upon the rood above the head of His blessed Son was the handwriting of ten ordinances given at Sinai. It was because this law had been broken in every point that Jesus poured out His blood, thus giving His life to redeem us from the curse of the law. And so all of our sins have been settled for. There the law, which we had so dishonored, has been magnified to the full in the satisfaction which He made to the divine justice. Thus Christ has become the "end of the law . . . to every one that believeth." It is, of course, the Jewish believers Paul has in mind when he says "us," for Gentiles were not under the law. But it is true now in principle for us all, to whom the knowledge of the law has come. Christ has, by His death, met every claim against us and canceled the bond we could not pay.

And now as a victorious leader He has come forth from the tomb, having made a prey of the evil principalities and powers who gloated over His apparent defeat when He was crucified through weakness, but who are now themselves defeated in His resurrection. He has ascended to heaven in a glorious triumph, having made a spectacle of them, openly triumphing over them in His cross.

> His be the Victor's name
> Who fought the fight alone,
> Triumphant saints no honor claim
> His conquest was their own.
>
> By weakness and defeat
> He won the meed and crown,
> Trod all our foes beneath His feet
> By being trodden down.

Bless, bless the Conqueror slain,
    Slain in His victory;
Who lived, who died, who lives again,
    For thee, His church, for thee.

He took our place upon the cross and now we share in all the results of that work. We are one with Him in the new creation. The law and all its ritual was given to man in the flesh. Christians are not in the flesh but in the Spirit, and the law, as such, has nothing to say to the man in this new sphere beyond the reach of death. And so he concludes this marvelous section with a solemn admonition not to permit ourselves to be disturbed by any who would put us back under the law in any shape or form. "Let no man therefore judge you in meat, or in drink, or in respect of an holyday, or of the new moon, or of the sabbath days." All these once had their place and he who would be an obedient child of the old covenant was called upon to observe the regulations regarding them scrupulously. All these, however, were but a shadow of things to come—things which have now come—"For the body is of Christ."

In the Old Testament dispensation the light of God was shining upon Christ, and all the forms and ceremonies, including even the weekly Sabbaths, were but shadows cast by Him. Since He Himself has come and fulfilled all the redemptive types the believer has "everything in Jesus, and Jesus everything." The very fact that He links the Sabbath with the other ceremonies shows clearly that the rule of life for the believer is not the ten words given at Sinai. While confessing this law to be holy, just, and good, the new creation man is not under it. He is, as Paul expresses it elsewhere, "under law to Christ," or more properly "en-lawed to Christ" (1 Cor. 9:21). That is, his responsibility now is to walk in fellowship with the risen Christ, the Head of the body of which he is but a feeble member in whom dwells the Holy Spirit to be the power of the new life—manifested in subjection to the exalted Lord.

None need fear that this will make for a lower standard of piety than if one were under the law as a rule of life. It is a far higher standard. He whose one thought and desire is to manifest the risen life of Christ in all his ways will lead a holier life than he who is seeking to subject the flesh to rules and regulations, even though given from heaven in a dispensation now past. This comes out very strongly in the contrast between the Sabbath of the law and the Lord's Day of the new creation. There is no commandment in the New Testament inculcating the sacredness of the first day of the week and demanding that Christians observe it scrupulously for holy purposes, yet the consensus of judgment of spiritually minded believers all through the centuries has led to the honoring of this day as a time of worship, meditation, and Christian testimony, which has given it a preeminence from a spiritual standpoint that the Jewish Sabbath never had.

Nor are we called upon to substitute a Christian ritual service for the Jewish ritual that we have discarded. We worship now by the Spirit of God whose delight it is to occupy the hearts of the redeemed with Him to whom they owe all their blessing. Thus all that is fleshly or carnal must give way, as but prefatory and evanescent, and that which is spiritual and abiding takes its place.

CHAPTER 9

CHRIST THE ANTIDOTE TO ORIENTAL MYSTICISM

Colossians 2:18–19

Let no man beguile you of your reward in a voluntary humility and worshipping of angels, intruding into those things which he hath not seen, vainly puffed up by his fleshly mind, and not holding the Head, from which all the body by joints and bands having nourishment ministered, and knit together, increaseth with the increase of God. (vv. 18–19)

The natural man is distinctly religious. He does not need to be regenerated in order to *feel* after God. While it is true of all the unsaved that "there is none that seeketh after God" in the sense of seeking Him for His own sake, yet it has been well said that man is incurably religious. He must have something to worship. And so Satan has supplied him with cults of all descriptions to suit every type of mind.

One of the oldest systems that has come down even to our own day is that of Parseeism, based upon the Zend Avesta, supposed to have originated with the Persian hero and prophet, Zoroaster, or Zarathustra, as he is called in the Persian scriptures. This system teaches a mystical dualism. Ahura Mazda, or Ormuzd, is the infinite God, the Eternal Light. A lesser deity, Ahriman, the Prince of Darkness, sometimes looked upon as the creator of matter, is in constant conflict with the supreme deity. For twelve thousand years he is destined to wage war against the light and then his kingdom of darkness will be destroyed.

This system permeated various schools of thought, and in apostolic days had been widely accepted throughout the Greek and Roman world under the name Mithraism. Its votaries went everywhere proclaiming it as the great unifying world religion. It was a vast secret society, its initiates going from one mystical degree to another until they became adepts.

This satanic system trembled before the advancing hosts of Christianity, and finally sought to combine certain of its views with a part of the Christian revelation. As we have already seen, by an eclectic combination of Judaism, Greek philosophy, and Oriental mysticism, a new religion was formed, divided, however, into many different sects all alike unsound as to Christ, and all rejecting the inspiration of the Holy Scripture and substituting the vain speculations of the human mind. Yet imitations of almost every Christian doctrine were found in some one or other of these systems, but with certain accretions and contradictions that made them most dangerous.

Justin Martyr wrote some years after the apostle John passed from this scene, "Many spirits are abroad in the world and the credentials they display are splendid gifts of mind, eloquence and logic. Christian, look carefully, and ask for the print of the nails." All these systems denied the true Christ of God who gave Himself for our sins upon the cross of shame. Some, like the Docetists, taught that the humanity of Jesus was simply an appearance, unreal and immaterial. The first epistle of John meets this in a very wonderful way.

Another sect, afterward headed up in Cerinthus, the great arch-heretic of the second century, called by Polycarp, "the firstborn of Satan," taught that Jesus was the natural son of Joseph and Mary, who died on the cross finally to separate himself from his own sin, but to whom the Christ (identified with the eternal Spirit) came at his baptism and illumination, but left him at the cross. This system seems to be particularly before the mind of the apostle Paul and he combats it in a masterly manner.

In all of these systems knowledge was given the preeminence over faith. The latter, which is confidence in revealed testimony, was repudiated by these theorists who assumed acquaintance with divine mysteries far beyond that of ordinary people and quite in advance of the biblical revelation. In their pride and folly they put a great number of spirit-beings, known as eons, between the soul and the unknowable God. These were all classified and named, as for instance,

Reason, Wisdom, Power, and similar divine attributes. All this appeals to the natural man. It sounds like humility to say, "In myself I am so utterly ignorant and unworthy, it is not for me to go directly to God the Father or to Christ the Son. I will therefore avail myself of mediating angels and spirits who can present my cause in a more suitable manner than I can myself." But it is really pride of intellect, and is the grossest unbelief, when God has declared that "there is . . . one mediator between God and men, the man Christ Jesus; who gave himself a ransom for all to be testified in due time." The lowly man will receive what He has made known in His Word.

Through the infinite mercy of God the early church triumphed largely over these satanic efforts to ally these dying cults and systems with Christianity. The Holy Spirit so clearly exposed that the church repudiated in one council after another these vile theories which would have made man his own Savior. But all down the centuries since there have been those who from time to time have taken up certain elements of these discarded schools of thought and sought to foist them upon Christians as though they were new and wonderful truths.

Romanism, with its doctrine of justification by works, purgatorial purification after death, and mediating saints and angels, has simply adopted much that the apostles refused, and palms it off on its credulous dupes as traditional Christianity. Imagine anyone praying to saints and angels, or adoring their images, with the solemn words before him of this eighteenth verse, "Let no man beguile you of your reward in a voluntary humility and worshipping of angels, intruding into those things which he hath not seen, vainly puffed up by his fleshly mind." How striking the contrast between the expressions "voluntary humility" and "vainly puffed up."

I recall a friend of my youth, a very gracious and kindly man, who had been brought up from childhood in the Roman communion, with whom I often sought to reason out of the Scripture in order to show him the simplicity of the gospel of Christ. I remember when I asked why he prayed to the blessed Virgin Mary instead of directly to our Lord Jesus how with an air of the greatest humility he answered, "Oh, I am too sinful, too utterly unworthy, to go directly to our blessed Lord. He is infinitely above me, so pure and holy. His majesty is so great that I would not dare to prostrate myself before Him. But I know that no one has such influence with a son as his mother. I know, too, that a pure woman's tender heart feels for sinners in their sorrows and failures, therefore I go to the blessed Virgin Mary and pour out my heart to her as to my own mother. I plead with her to speak for me to her holy, spotless Son, and I feel sure that she will influence Him as no other could." This sounds like lowliness of mind and humility of spirit. It is really the most subtle kind of pride, for it involves proposing to be wiser than the revealed Word of God.

There, as we have seen, we read of only the "one mediator." We learn that "the Father sent the Son to be the Saviour of the world," that "he bore our sins in his own body on the tree," that His tender heart was filled with compassion for sinners here on earth. None were too vile or degraded but that they were invited to come to Him. The worst His enemies could say of Him was, "This man receiveth sinners, and eateth with them." And up there in yonder glory He is the same Jesus that He was when here on earth. We may rest assured that "we have not an High Priest which cannot be touched with the feeling of our infirmities, but One who was tempted in all points like as we are, apart from sin" (author's translation), and who is "able to succour those who are tempted."

In His name we are bidden to "come boldly unto the throne of grace, that we may obtain mercy, and find grace for [seasonable] help." Why turn aside to angels or saints, however devoted, or even to His blessed mother herself, when we can go directly to Him, assured of His deep interest in all that concerns us? He made intercession for transgressors on the cross; up there at God's right hand He ever lives to make intercession for those who trust in Him. And so it is not an evidence of humility to say, I am too unworthy to go to Christ. It is only unbelief that would lead one thus to speak. He stands with arms outstretched, pleading with all who are in trouble or distress, "Come unto me, all ye that labour and are heavy laden, and I will give you rest." What base ingratitude to turn from Him to any other! What amazing folly to think it necessary to have anyone speak for me to Him, when He stands there showing His wounded hands and saying, "Peace be unto you." It is only pride and unbelief that would put Him off at a distance and bring angels in between.

This voluntary humility and worshiping of angels is in itself a complete denial of the new creation. It fails to recognize the wondrous truth that all believers are one body with their exalted Head. And so the apostle goes on to say, "And not holding the Head, from which all the body by joints and bands having nourishment ministered, and knit together, increaseth with the increase of God." "Holding the Head" is recognizing our link with Him, both in life and by the Spirit. He, the exalted One at God's right hand, is the source of blessing for all His people in this scene. As of old the holy oil poured upon Aaron's head "went down to the skirts of his garment" (Ps. 133:2), so now from the Head in heaven blessing in the Spirit's power comes down to every member of His body on the earth.

It will be observed that the figure of a body is not merely that of a society or, as we would say, an organization. It is far more wonderful than that. It is a divine organism. Just as truly as all the members of a human body form the complete man, so do all believers in Christ, through the Spirit's baptism, form the one new man. See in this connection 1 Corinthians 12:12–13 and Ephesians 2:15. If out of touch with the Head through failure to apprehend the intimacy of our relation to Him we put anything or any creature between ourselves and Him, we are not holding the Head. Satan knows, as one has well put it, that if he could get but the thickness of a sheet of paper between the Head and the body, all life would be destroyed. This, of course, can never be, but it is sadly possible so utterly to misunderstand our relation to the Head, and so fail to avail ourselves of the supplies of grace that might be ours did we but walk in fellowship with Him, that we would be out of communion with Him and therefore not consciously guided by Him.

We are told that from the Head all the body is nourished, and this through the ministry of joints and bands placed in the body for this very purpose by the Holy Spirit, so that all being knit together grows, or increases, with the increase of God. This is most blessedly expanded and elaborated in Ephesians 4:11–16. There we see how the risen Lord has given various gifts to His church for the perfecting of the saints with a view to the work of the ministry for the edifying of the body of Christ. Note specially verses 15–16 where we are told that He would have us "grow up into him in all things, which is the head, even Christ: from whom the whole body fitly joined together and compacted by that which every joint supplieth, according to the effectual working in the measure of every part, maketh increase of the body unto the edifying of itself in love." What a marvelous picture is this, and how strikingly does the one passage complement the other, and what responsibility does it put upon each one of us as members of Christ and members one of another!

There are no useless members in this body. Just as in the human body every joint, every ligament, every hidden part, has some service to perform for the good of the whole, even though as yet physicians and surgeons may not fully understand the need of every gland and organ. Though they may speak, as some do, of certain useless parts or discarded vestiges of earlier forms, yet we may be very sure that God in His infinite wisdom has a use for every member of the body. So in the mystical body of Christ let no believer think of himself as useless, as without any special gift, and therefore as having no part in the building up of the whole.

There is one term used in 1 Corinthians 12:28 that is most suggestive. It is the little word *helps*. Notice how it is sandwiched in between gifts of healings and governments. We may not all have spectacular gifts, but we can all be helps. The apostle writing to one church says, "Ye all being helpers together by prayer." Here is a service the feeblest saint may perform for the benefit of the whole body.

If in spiritual health each member will function aright for the edification of all; but just as in the natural order diseased members become a menace to the entire body, so Christians out of fellowship with God, in a low or carnal state, are hindrances where they should be helpers. May each one of us be concerned about our responsibility here. May we be so occupied with our blessed, glorified Head, so careful to see that there is nothing interfering with our communion with Him, that He may be able to use us as joints or bands to minister nourishment and blessing to His people that all may be the more knit together because of our faithfulness in seeking to be helpers of one another's faith, that thus the body may indeed increase with the increase of God.

And now, in closing, let me say a word to my younger brethren in Christ who seek to preach the gospel or to minister for the edification of believers. Bear in mind that if you would be true ministers of Jesus Christ you are to preach the Word and seek to occupy your hearers with the truth of God. Do not, I beg of you, give way to a very common vanity of preachers—speculation in regard to things not revealed. You are not sent forth to acquaint men with unsubstantiated theories nor to occupy their minds with speculative systems. God has entrusted you with His own holy Word, and He holds you responsible to give that out in all its clearness and simplicity. One "Thus saith the Lord" is worth a ton of human thoughts and ideas. Unreliable theological disquisitions and philosophical discussions never saved one poor sinner or comforted a discouraged saint. It is the truth of God, ministered in the power of the Holy Spirit, that alone can accomplish this. All else is but wasting precious time and is dishonoring to the Lord who sent you out to proclaim His truth.

This divinely given message ministered in the power of the Holy Spirit sent down from heaven will awaken the careless, quicken the dead in trespasses and sins, give peace to the anxious, comfort the distressed, and sanctify believers. To substitute the empty dreams of carnal or unregenerate men for this, is the utmost folly. Of old, God said, through Jeremiah, "The prophet that hath a dream, let him tell a dream; and he that hath my word, let him speak my word faithfully. What is the chaff to the wheat? saith the LORD" (Jer. 23:28).

To add to His Word is but to pervert it. Neither tradition, nor the voice of the church, nor yet fancied superior intellectual illumination can complete that which is already perfect—the revelation of the mind of God in His holy Word. "The Bible and the Bible alone" is the foundation of our faith.

CHAPTER 10

CHRIST THE ANTIDOTE
TO CARNAL ASCETICISM

Colossians 2:20–23

Wherefore if ye be dead with Christ from the rudiments of the world, why, as though living in the world, are ye subject to ordinances, (touch not; taste not; handle not; which all are to perish with the using;) after the commandments and doctrines of men? Which things have indeed a show of wisdom in will worship. and humility, and neglecting of the body; not in any honour to the satisfying of the flesh. (vv. 20–23)

It is a great mistake and a fatal blunder into which the best of people readily fall to fail to distinguish the two very different senses in which the term "the flesh" is used in the Bible. Sometimes it refers solely to our bodies, "this mortal flesh," but in the doctrinal parts of the New Testament it generally means the nature that fallen man has inherited from his first father. God created man, we are told, in His own image, "in the likeness of God made he him; male and female created he them; . . . and called their name Adam, in the day when they were created" (Gen. 5:1–2). Physically perfect, they were morally innocent and spiritually like unto God, who is a Spirit and the Father of spirits.

But in the very next verse we read, "Adam . . . begat a son in his own likeness, and after his image" (Gen. 5:3). This was after sin had defiled his nature and poisoned the springs of life, and all his children now bear this fallen image and likeness. Hence the need of regeneration, and so our Lord said to Nicodemus, "That which is born of the flesh is flesh, and that which is born of the Spirit is spirit." He is not merely saying that that which is born of the physical body is a physical body, but that personality which comes into the world through natural generation and birth is one with the fallen nature that Adam acquired when he fell. This is called distinctively, "the flesh," "the body of the flesh," "sin in the flesh," "sin that dwelleth in us," "the carnal mind which is not subject to the law of God, neither indeed can be"; and is the nature of the old man—the unregenerate natural man.

We are told that we all were by nature children of wrath, even as others. When converted, or regenerated, this carnal nature is not altered in the slightest degree. It is never improved nor sanctified, either in whole or in part. In the cross of Christ God has condemned it utterly as too vile for improvement. The believer has received a new nature which is spiritual, the nature of the new man. He is now responsible to walk in obedience to the Word of God, which appeals only to this new nature. The old and the new natures are in the believer and will be until the redemption of the body.

It is true that the flesh, or the old nature, acts through the members of the body, but the body itself is not evil. Every natural instinct or physical appetite, no matter how perfectly right and proper it may be, and used as God intended, may be perverted to selfish and dishonorable purposes. But we are called upon to mortify, or put to death, the deeds of the body and no longer to yield our members as instruments of unrighteousness unto sin, but to present the body with all its ransomed powers unto God to be used for His service under the controlling power of His Holy Spirit. Hence the Christian is called to a life of self-abnegation and so the apostle Paul could say, "I keep under my body, and bring it into subjection."

But by that he does not mean that he visits needless punishment upon his physical flesh in order to purify his spirit, but rather that he does not permit unlawful or inordinate physical appetites to dominate him, and so lead him into excesses which would bring dishonor upon the ministry committed to him and upon the name of the Lord whose servant he is. This subjection of the body will ever be necessary as long as we are in this scene of testing. So the apostle Peter tells us, "He that hath suffered in the flesh hath ceased from sin." It is not that we obtain deliverance from the power of sin by ascetic practices such as flagellation, fasting, or ignoring physical comfort, but rather by refusing obedience to carnal impulses, the gratification of which may give physical pleasure while they war against the soul.

And in this we may see the contrast between our Lord's temptation and our own. Of Him we read that "he suffered being tempted." Of us, that we cease from sin if we suffer in the flesh. In other words, to Him, the Holy One, temptation caused the keenest suffering. His holy nature shrank from the slightest contact with evil even in satanic suggestion. But with us, fallen as we are, the suggestion of evil may be seductively pleasing, and we must resolutely refuse the thought of sensual pleasure in order that we may walk in purity before God. "He was tempted in all things like as we are, apart from sin." That is, He was never tempted by inward desire for sin. He could say, "The prince of this world cometh and hath nothing in me." With us it is far otherwise. When temptation is presented from without we are sadly conscious of the fact that we have a traitor within who would open the door of the fortress to the enemy if he were not carefully watched. And right here is where purpose of heart is needed in order that we may cleave to the Lord and give no ground to the suggestions of the flesh or the promptings of the Adversary.

An Indian, in explaining the conflict of the two natures, said, "It seems to me as though two dogs are fighting within me: one is a black dog, and he is very savage and very bad. The other is a white dog, and he is very gentle and very good. But the black dog fights with him all the time." "And which dog wins?" someone asked. Laconically the Indian replied, "Which ever one I say 'sic him' to." And it was well put, for if the will is on the side of the evil, the flesh will triumph; but if the will is subdued by grace and subject to the Holy Spirit, the new nature will control.

It is for lack of understanding this important truth that many have supposed they could perfect themselves in holiness by imposing penances and suffering of various kinds upon the body. At a very early day such views came into the church. The Jewish Essenes and the Stoic philosophers had accustomed both Jews and Gentiles to the thought that the body in itself is evil and must be subdued if one would advance in holiness. These views were taken up by certain sects of Gnostics, while others went to the opposite extreme and taught that the spiritual alone was important, and that the body might be used in any way without polluting the soul.

But in these last four verses of our present chapter the apostle warns against the folly of seeking holiness through asceticism. He describes these practices as being part of that philosophy of which he has already spoken in verse 8, which he designated the rudiments or elements of the world. Challenging the believer, as a new man in Christ, who died with Him to his old place and condition in the world, he asks: "Wherefore if ye [died] with Christ from the [elements] of the world, why, as though living in the world, are ye subject to ordinances, . . . after the commandments and doctrines of men?" I have purposely left out certain parenthetical expressions which we will look at in a moment.

The great thing now to see is that all these rules and regulations for the sub-duing of the body are according to the principles of the world. They all take for granted that God is still trying in some way to improve the flesh, and this we know is not His purpose. Through John the Baptist He said, "The axe is laid to the root of the tree." Not only in modern times, but in those early days of Chris-tianity that we are considering, men have laid the axe, or the pruning-knife, if you will, to the fruit of the tree as though the tree might be improved if the bad fruit were cut off. Get men to reform, to sign pledges, to put themselves under rules and regulations, to starve the body, to inflict physical suffering upon it, and surely its vile propensities will be at least annulled if not eliminated, and little by little men will become spiritual and godlike. The formula which thousands have taken up within the last few years:

> Every day, in every way,
> I am getting better and better,

expresses the mind of many. But no amount of self-control, no physical suffering whatsoever can change the carnal mind, called emphatically, "the flesh."

Saint Jerome tells how, having lived a lecherous life in his youth, after he became a Christian he fled from all contact with the gross and vulgar world in which he had once sought to gratify every fleshly desire. He left Rome and wandered to Palestine, and there lived in a cave near Bethlehem where he sought to subdue his carnal nature by fasting almost to starvation. And then he tells us how disappointed he was when, exhausted and weary, he fell asleep and dreamed he was still rioting among the dissolute companions of his godless days. The flesh cannot be starved into subjection. It cannot be improved by subjecting it to ordinances whether human or divine. But as we walk in the Spirit, and are occupied thus with the risen Christ, we are delivered from the power of fleshly lusts that war against the soul.

In the parenthetical portion of verses 21–22 the apostle gives us a sample, if we may so say, of the carnal ordinances or doctrines of men to which he refers, "Touch not; taste not; handle not." He is not saying, Do not touch, taste, or handle these ascetic regulations—that would be nonsense—but these are the human rules, through obedience to which the ascetic hoped to attain to a higher degree of spirituality. How often we have heard verse 21 quoted as though for the guidance of Christians today, exactly the opposite of that which the apostle intended. All such regulations are to perish with the using.

These things have, indeed, an appearance of wisdom in will worship and humility and neglecting of the body, or punishing the body by making it suffer. It is natural to suppose that such things would have a tendency to free one from carnal desires, but untold thousands of monks, hermits, and ascetics of all descriptions, have proved that they are useless against the indulgence of the flesh. One may shut himself up in a monastery in order to escape the world, only to find he has taken the world in with him. One may dwell in a cave in the desert in order to subdue the flesh, only to find that the more the body is weakened and neglected, the more powerful the flesh becomes.

Dr. A. T. Robertson translates the last part of verse 20: "Why, as though living in the world, do you dogmatize; such as, Touch not; taste not; handle not?" These rules may be elevated to the importance of dogmas, but they will never enable one to achieve the object he has in view.

You have heard of the man who, anxious to fit himself for the presence of God and awakened to a sense of the emptiness of a life of worldly pleasure, fled from the city to the desert and made his home in a cave in the rocks, there practicing the greatest austerities, and hoping through prayer and penance to reach the place where he would be acceptable to God. Hearing of another hermit who was reputed to be a very holy and devout man, he made a long, wearisome journey across the desert, supported only by his staff, in order to interview him and learn from him how he might find peace with God. In answer to his agonized questions the aged anchorite said to him, "Take that staff, that dry rod which is in your hand, plant it in the desert soil, water it daily, offering fervent prayers as you do so, and when it bursts into leaf and bloom you may know that you have made your peace with God."

Rejoicing that at last he had what seemed like authoritative instruction in regard to this greatest of all ventures, he hastened back to his cell and planted his rod as he had been told to do. For long, weary days, weeks, and months, he faithfully watered the dry stick and prayed for the hour when the token of his acceptance would be manifest. At last one day, in utter despair and brokenness of spirit, weakened by fasting and sick with longing for the apparently unattainable, he exclaimed bitterly, "It is all no use. I am no better today than I was when I first came to the desert. The fact is, I am just like this dry stick myself.

It needs life before there can be leaves and fruit, and I need life, for I am dead in my sins and cannot produce fruit for God." And then it seemed as though a voice within said, "At last you have learned the lesson that the old hermit meant to teach you. It is because you are dead and have no strength or power in yourself that you must turn to Christ alone and find life and peace in Him." And leaving his desert cave he went back to the city to find the Word of God and in its sacred pages learn the way of peace.

And let us remember it is as impossible to obtain holiness by ascetic practices as it is to buy salvation by physical suffering. We are saved in the first place, not through anything we undergo, but through that which our blessed Lord Jesus Christ underwent for us on Calvary's cross, and, blessed be God, He who died for us upon that cross now lives for us at God's right hand, and He is the power for holiness as well as for justification. By the Holy Spirit He dwells within us, and as we yield ourselves unto God as those who are alive from the dead, He is enabled to live out His wondrous life in us. Does your heart sometimes cry:

> Tell me what to do to be pure
>   In the sight of all-seeing eyes;
> Tell me is there no thorough cure,
>   No escape from the sins I despise?
> Will my Saviour only pass by,
>   Only show how faulty I've been?
> Will He not attend to my cry?
>   May I not this moment be clean?

Oh, believe me, dear, anxious, seeking Christian, you will find holiness in the same Christ in whom you found salvation. As you cease from self-occupation and look up in faith to Him you will be transformed into His own glorious image. You will become like Him as you gaze on His wonderful face. There is no other way by which the flesh may be subdued and your life become one of triumph over the power of sin. Asceticism is but a vain will-o'-the-wisp that, while it promises you victory, will plunge you into the morass of disappointment and defeat. But occupation with Christ risen at God's right hand is the sure way to overcome the lusts of the flesh and to become like Him who has said, "For their sakes I sanctify myself, that they also may be sanctified through the truth."

Of Him they said He was a glutton and a wine-bibber, because He came not as an ascetic but as a Man among men, entering with them into every sinless experience of human life. He has "left us an example that we should follow His steps." He has come to sanctify every natural relationship, not to do violence to those affections and feelings which He Himself implanted in the hearts of mankind.

CHAPTER 11

CHRIST THE BELIEVER'S LIFE AND OBJECT

Colossians 3:1–4

If ye then be risen with Christ, seek those things which are above, where Christ sitteth on the right hand of God. Set your affection on things above, not on things on the earth. For ye are dead, and your life is hid with Christ in God. When Christ, who is our life, shall appear, then shall ye also appear with him in glory. (vv. 1–4)

After the somewhat lengthy digression of verses 13–23 in the previous chapter, the apostle comes back to apply the truth taught in verse 12. I think we shall get the connection better if we read these two passages without anything intervening: "Buried with him in baptism, wherein also ye are risen with him through the faith of the operation of God, who hath raised him from the dead. . . . If ye then be risen with Christ, seek those things which are above, where Christ sitteth on the right hand of God." All that has come in between these two verses was in the nature of warning against false systems that would have robbed the believer of this great truth of unity with Christ in death and resurrection.

It is of all importance that we realize that we do not stand before God on the ground of responsibility. The responsible man failed utterly to keep his obligations. There was nothing for him, therefore, but condemnation, but our Lord Jesus Christ has borne that condemnation. He voluntarily, in infinite grace, took the place of the sinner and bore his judgment upon the cross. Now in resurrection, as we have seen, all who believe are not only given a perfect representation by Him before the throne of God, but we are in Him in virtue of being partakers of His life. "In Adam" meant that we were born of his race. "In Christ," in contrast, clearly indicates that we have received a new life from Him and, therefore, we are not to think of ourselves as in any sense on probation. All that was ended on the cross of Christ.

> Jesus died and we died with Him,
>   Buried in His grave we lay,
> One in Him in resurrection,
>   Soon with Him in heaven's bright day.
>
> Death and judgment are behind us,
>   Grace and glory are before;
> All the billows rolled o'er Jesus,
>   There exhausted all their power.

It is when the soul enters into this experimentally, realizing that the death of Christ, in which faith has given him part, has severed the link that bound him to the world and all its purposes and has freed him from all necessity to be subject to sin in the flesh, that he will be free to glorify God as he walks in newness of life. Most theological systems fail to apprehend this great truth of the new man in Christ, hence so few believers have settled peace and realize their union with Him who sits at God's right hand, not only as the Head of the church, but as the Head of every person who has found life through Him.

Occupation, then, with Christ risen in the energy of the Holy Spirit, is the power for holiness. We are called upon to seek those things which are above, where Christ sits on the right hand of God. Our real life is there, our truest, best interests are all identified with Him. Heavenly-mindedness is the natural, or I should say, spiritual outcome of this realization. As the heart is taken up with Him, we will be concerned about representing Him aright in this world where He is still rejected and His claims refused.

The marginal reading of verse 2 is better than the text of the King James

Version: "Set your mind on things above, not on things on the earth." That is, as a watch is set to the sun in order to mark the time correctly, so let your mind be set to Christ risen in order that His life may be seen in you. This is in contrast to the things spoken of in Philippians 3:19: "Who mind earthly things." The time for this is past for those who are now one with Christ risen. This will not make us impractical and visionary, but we shall live all the more consistently thus fulfilling our varied responsibilities in the home, in business, in the state, and, of course, in the church, as our minds are fixed on heavenly things. This is indeed the "ribbon of blue" to which reference was made in an earlier address.

We will manifest the heavenly character, just where we come closest into contact with the things of the earth. I think we may see in Christ during the forty days between resurrection and ascension something of what this involves. He was still here upon the earth but He was altogether heavenly. "Though we have known Christ after the flesh, yet now henceforth know we him so no more," and we are called into association with Him to manifest the heavenly character as we walk the desert sands. Men of the world will not understand this, and we need not expect them to. But nevertheless they can and will recognize and appreciate true piety and Christian character even though they hate those who possess it, as Cain hated Abel because his own works were evil and his brother's righteous. But it should be true of us, as of our blessed Lord Himself, that this hatred is undeserved, according as it was written of Him, "They hated Me without a cause."

The third verse epitomizes this in a very wonderful way, "For ye [have died], and your life is hid with Christ in God." We have died to all that we once were as children of Adam, and now we do not have independent life as Christians, but Christ Himself is our life and, while it is true we have this eternal life abiding in us, He who is the source and sustainer of it is hidden yonder in the heavens "in God," and so our life is safe in His keeping. One can understand and appreciate the rather crude expression of the simple brother who, after his conversion, had been greatly concerned lest by some sinful act or lack of faith he might in some way forfeit his salvation and lose the new life given in grace. But as he listened to an address upon these wonderful words of this third verse, his anxiety disappeared and he exclaimed with rapture, "Glory to God! Whoever heard of a man drowning with his head that high above water!" Admitting all their crudity, his words nevertheless expressed a great truth. Our Head is in heaven, our life is in Him, hidden in God, therefore we are eternally one with Him and nothing can ever separate the Christian from the risen Christ.

Outwardly, believers in the Lord Jesus are like other men, they are still in dying bodies, and often distressed by the flesh within and in conflict with Satan and the world without, yet each believer is to walk through this scene in the power of resurrection life, manifesting his union with his glorified Head. He is called to be a man of God, though in the humblest condition of life.

> There is no glory halo
>   Round his devoted head,
> No lustre marks the sacred path
>   In which his footsteps tread.
>
> But holiness is graven
>   Upon his thoughtful brow,
> And all his steps are ordered
>   In the light of heaven e'en now.
>
> He often is peculiar,
>   And oft misunderstood,
> And yet his power is felt by all—
>   The evil and the good.
>
> For he doth live in touch with heaven
>   A life of faith and prayer;
> His hope, his purpose and his all,
>   His life is centered there.

This is indeed to be a consistent member of the body of Christ, manifestly displaying the character of the new man whose Head is in heaven. And, though like his Lord despised and rejected of men, the Christian is called to run with patience the race set before him, knowing that the day of manifestation is nearing when he, too, according to his measure, shall see of the travail of his soul and be satisfied. Christ will find His satisfaction in us, we will find ours in Him.

> He and I in that bright glory
>   One deep joy will share;
> Mine to be forever with Him,
>   His that I am there.

And when the day of the Lord dawns after earth's long, dark night—or, to put it in another way, after man's garish day is ended—then those who are content to be strangers and pilgrims here during His rejection, shall shine forth with Him when He comes to reign as King of kings and Lord of lords. And so we read in verse 4, "When Christ, who is our life, shall appear, then shall we also appear with him in glory." We might read, "be manifested" for "appear"—it would perhaps make the thought even clearer. When He with whom we have died and in whom we are risen shall return from heaven and be manifested before His earthly people who will be waiting for Him in that day, and before His foes as well, then we also shall be manifested with Him in glory.

As we think of His coming, we know it is presented to us in two aspects in the New Testament, and perhaps, that which appeals most to every real lover of Christ is what we commonly call "the rapture." Our hearts long for the hour when "the Lord himself shall descend from heaven with a shout, with the voice of the archangel, and with the trump of God: and the dead in Christ shall rise first, and we which are alive and remain shall be caught up together with them in the clouds, to meet the Lord in the air." We think of this as the end of the race, and as the time, too, when "He will change these bodies of our humiliation and make them like unto the body of His glory," when "this mortal shall put on immortality and this corruptible shall put on incorruption," and we shall be fully "conformed to the image of God's Son." This will be the fulfillment of our Lord's promise given before He went away: "I go to prepare a place for you. And if I go and prepare a place for you, I will come again, and receive you unto myself; that where I am, there ye may be also." This will be the occasion of our reception into the Father's house.

But all of this, blessed as it is, and calculated to stir the souls of His waiting ones to their deepest depths, is but an introduction to the glories yet to be revealed in the everlasting kingdom of our Lord and Savior Jesus Christ. He is coming back to the earth that rejected Him, and all His saints are coming with Him not, of course, to take up human conditions here in the world again, but in resurrection bodies to appear with Him before the astonished eyes of those who still reject Him, and to the delight of those who will be waiting for Him as the delivering King in that day when the word will be fulfilled, "Behold, he cometh with clouds; and every eye shall see him, and they also which pierced him: and all the tribes of the land shall wail because of him." That will be the time when we shall appear with Him in glory.

To this the apostle refers again in 2 Thessalonians 1:5–11 where he comforts the suffering saints with the assurance that tribulation will be recompensed to those that trouble them, and rest will be the portion of the redeemed. "When the

Lord Jesus shall be revealed from heaven with his mighty angels, in flaming fire taking vengeance on them that know not God, and that obey not the gospel of our Lord Jesus Christ: who shall be punished with everlasting destruction from the presence of the Lord, and from the glory of his power; when He shall come to be glorified in his saints, and to be admired in all them that believe . . . in that day." I have purposely omitted the parenthetical words, "because our testimony among you was believed." They explain why any from among earth's inhabitants will be associated with Christ in the glory of that revelation.

> Lamb of God, Thou soon in glory
> Wilt to this sad earth return;
> All Thy foes shall quake before Thee,
> All that now despise Thee, mourn.
>
> Then shall we, at Thine appearing,
> With Thee in Thy kingdom reign;
> Thine the praise and Thine the glory,
> Lamb of God for sinners slain!

This is the consummation to which the Christian dispensation is tending, when the kingdoms of this world shall become the kingdoms of our God and of His Christ, and His one-time pilgrim people shall reign with Him in righteousness throughout Messiah's glorious years.

And with this the apostle completes the doctrinal teaching of the epistle to the Colossians. In these first two chapters with which the four opening verses of chapter 3 are linked, he has unfolded in a marvelous way the truth of the new creation and our link with the risen Man, God's firstborn Son, the Heir of all things. We have seen that in Him we have deliverance from the power of darkness, and we are even now translated into His spiritual kingdom. In Him we have redemption, the forgiveness of sins, and have been made meet to be partakers of the inheritance of the saints in light. He has made peace by the blood of His cross, and we have been reconciled to God through His death.

We are now members of His mystical body and thus members one of another, called upon to hold the Head and in all things to be subject to Him as we pursue our way in faith through the wilderness of this world. Christ Himself is to be our heart's blessed object. He is the Antidote for every form of error, for in Him all the fullness of the Godhead dwells, and our fullness is found alone in Him. We have been identified with Him in His death, burial, and resurrection. All that was against us He has taken out of the way, paying our bond and nailing it to His cross. He Himself is now to be the portion of our souls. As we are occupied with Him, the risen One, with mind and heart set on heavenly things, we shall manifest His life here on earth while we wait for His return, when we shall be manifested with Him in glory.

What a gospel! Surely it was never conceived in the mind of man. It could not be, for it makes nothing of man but everything of Christ. May our hearts enter into it more and more as the days grow darker and the end draws near, "While we look not at the things that are seen, but at the things which are not seen," and live in daily expectation of His return to take us to be with Himself and make us fully like Himself forevermore.

> For God has fixed the happy day,
>   When the last tear shall dim our eyes,
> When He will wipe these tears away,
>   And fill our hearts with glad surprise.
> To hear His voice, and see His face,
>   And know the fulness of His grace.

This blessed consummation of all our hopes is set clearly before us in the Word of God as our goal—in order that, cheered by the glory shining from the gates of the city, we may be heartened and lifted above discouragement, and the depressing power of present sorrows, whether in the world or the church, so that we may run the race with patience, ever "looking unto Jesus."

PART 2

PRACTICAL

CHAPTER 12

Practical Holiness by Conformity to Christ in Relation to Ourselves

Colossians 3:5–11

Mortify therefore your members which are upon the earth; fornication, uncleanness, inordinate affection, evil concupiscence, and covetousness, which is idolatry: for which things' sake the wrath of God cometh on the children of disobedience: in the which ye also walked some time, when ye lived in them. But now ye also put off all these; anger, wrath, malice, blasphemy, filthy communication out of your mouth. Lie not one to another, seeing that ye have put off the old man with his deeds; and have put on the new man, which is renewed in knowledge after the image of him that created him: where there is neither Greek nor Jew, circumcision nor uncircumcision, Barbarian, Scythian, bond nor free: but Christ is all, and in all. (vv. 5–11)

W e come now to the consideration of the practical teaching of the epistle where we have emphasized for us the importance of walking in the power of the truth of the new man and our relationship to Christ as Head. And in this section, which includes verses 5–17 and is too lengthy to be taken up in one address, we have, first, that which relates to ourselves, our individual judgment of the old ways, in verses 5–11, which we will consider at this time. Then in verses 12–17, we have rather our relationship to others, particularly our brethren in Christ; or, as we might put it, the claims of Christian fellowship. We must be right ourselves, in our own inner lives, if we would be right toward others. "Keep thy heart with all diligence, for out of it are the issues of life." What I am when alone in the presence of God is what I really am. What I am before my fellows should be the outcome of this, otherwise my public life will be largely a sham.

There is a very suggestive lesson along this line in connection with the fine linen in the tabernacle. The tabernacle, as we know, was primarily a wonderful type of our Lord Jesus Christ. It was God's dwelling place; and we read, "The Word became flesh and tabernacled among us, and we beheld His glory, the glory as of the Only Begotten of the Father, full of grace and truth" (author's translation). Surrounding the court of the tabernacle were curtains of fine twined linen suspended from pillars. The fine linen, we learn from Revelation 19, is "the righteous acts of the saints" (literal rendering). Therefore the fine linen surrounding the court would speak of the perfect ways of our Lord Jesus Christ as displayed before men on earth. The hangings of the court were visible to all who drew near. But inside, covering the upright boards of the tabernacle, which were of acacia wood overlaid with gold, were ten curtains also of fine twined linen. These were not visible to men on the outside; they were seen by God Himself and, in measure, by His ministering priests. So if the fine linen outside speaks of Christ's righteousness as Man on earth visible to the eyes of other men, which led them to exclaim, "He hath done all things well," and which caused even Pilate to declare, "I find no fault in him," the ten curtains inside would speak of His perfect righteousness as seen by God the Father, that perfection which caused Him to open the heavens and proclaim, "This is my beloved Son in whom I have found all my delight."

Now how many cubits of fine twined linen were there forming the wall of the court? We learn that the court was 100 cubits long and 50 cubits wide. Subtracting 20 cubits for the varicolored gate of the tabernacle, we have 280 cubits, 100 on each side, 50 in the rear, and 30 in front. Inside there were ten curtains joined together, and each one was 28 cubits long. Here then we have another 280 cubits. Note this well. There were 280 cubits of fine twined linen surrounding the court

where all could behold it, and 280 cubits of fine twined linen forming the tabernacle itself, where only the eye of God saw it in its completeness! How suggestive
is all this, and what a lesson for us. Our blessed Lord was just the same before
God as before men. But the fact that the width of the curtains was different to
that of the hangings is also suggestive. The curtains were four cubits wide, and
four is the number of weakness, and speaks of Christ's perfect subjection to the
will of the Father. The hangings were five cubits wide, and five, we know, is the
number of responsibility, and suggests our Lord's taking the place of responsibility
here on earth, as meeting every claim of God that man had flouted. When His
enemies came asking, "Who art Thou?" He answered, "Altogether what I have
said unto you." With Him profession and life were in perfect agreement, and
this is the standard which God now puts before the believer.

Recognizing, then, our union with Christ, we are called upon to manifest His life.
There must be first of all the judgment of the old ways in their totality. In chapter
2 we have learned of our identification with Him in His death; in the cross we were
circumcised with the circumcision of Christ, therefore we are to mortify, or put to
death, our members which are upon the earth. The believer is never told to crucify
himself; he is told to mortify the members of his body. We have been crucified
with Christ. Faith lays hold of this, and so it is written: "They that are Christ's
have crucified the flesh with its affections and lusts." All passed under judgment in
the cross, but in order to make this practical the flesh must be kept, by faith, in the
place of death and its evil promptings refused in self-judgment.

The apostle insists first of all upon the importance of dealing unsparingly with
the sins that were so common in the heathen world out of which these Colossians had been saved. Sins, alas, almost as common in the world today, in spite
of increased light and civilization. The believer, recognizing his link with Christ,
is to abhor all uncleanness. He is to remember that the body is for the Lord,
and the Lord for the body, consequently every tendency to the sins mentioned
in verse 5—fornication, lasciviousness, inordinate affection, evil concupiscence
(or, unlawful lusts) and covetousness, which is idolatry (for in reality it is the
worship of self)—all these are to be judged in the light of the cross of Christ at
no matter what cost. No excuse must be offered for such sins nor any palliation
of their wickedness attempted on the ground of the innate tendencies of human
nature. These things are abhorrent to God and abhorrent to the new nature in
every believer, and because of them the wrath of God is coming on the children
of disobedience; as of old, when God destroyed the antediluvian world because
of corruption and violence, and rained fire from heaven upon the cities of the
plain because of unbridled lusts and passions.

In these sins, so characteristic of men away from God, the Colossians had once walked, living in them unblushingly, but that was before they knew Christ. Now, as risen with Him, these things, seen at last in their true light, must be refused as dishonoring to God and contrary to Christ. Other sins there are which in the eyes of many are far less vile and abominable than those mentioned above, but these, too, are to be put off. They were the habits of the old man, his old clothes, which are not fit to adorn the new man. And so we read, "But now ye also put off all these; anger, wrath, malice, blasphemy, filthy communication out of your mouth. Lie not one to another, seeing that ye have put off the old man with his deeds." The old man is more than the old nature. It is the man of old, the man you used to be before you knew Christ as Savior and Lord. In other words, the old man is all that I once was as an unsaved person. I am through with that man. He has disappeared, for faith, in the cross of Christ. But if I make this profession, let me be sure that I do not manifest his ways. Sometimes those who make the loudest professions in regard to the truth of the new creation are the poorest performers of the truth, and thus they give the lie to what they say by what they do. It was Emerson, I think, who said, "What you are speaks so loudly I cannot hear what you say." It is to be feared that many a Christian has lost his testimony because of carelessness here.

Anger, which, as we know from Ephesians 4:26, may be righteous, is generally but the raging of the flesh, and even where it is warranted (and we read of our blessed Lord looking round about upon His opponents with anger because of the hardness of their hearts), still this must not be nursed or it will degenerate into wrath, which is a settled condition of ill feeling toward an offender and generally has coupled with it a desire for revenge, and so malice springs from it. We have three generations of sin here: anger cherished begets wrath, and wrath if not judged begets malice. No matter how grievously I have been wronged, I am not to give place to the Devil and malign, or seek to harm, the one against whom I may have been righteously indignant in the beginning. "Let not the sun go down upon your wrath, neither give place to the devil."

Blasphemy—this dreadful sin may be either Godward or manward. To impute evil to God or to seek to misrepresent Him, or to pervert the truth as to the Father, the Son, or the Spirit, these are various ways in which men blaspheme against God. But to speak injuriously of one another, to circulate wicked and untruthful reports against one's brethren, to revile rulers or governors, or to seek to harm, by evil report, servants of God, all these are included under the general term blasphemy, and here how often have sharp-tongued religious controversialists failed even at the very moment that they were endeavoring to meet the blasphemy of their opponents in regard to divine things. When the hyper-Calvinist, the father of William Hone, the one-time infidel, described John Wesley as a child of the Devil because of his Arminianism, he had himself fallen into the sin of blasphemy. No wonder his son turned from such Christianity in horror, and was for years in darkness, until reached by divine grace. Railing accusations ill become those who have been saved through mercy alone and have occasion daily to confess their own sins and sue for divine forgiveness. The wrath of man works not the righteousness of God, and He, the Holy One, is not served by our hard speeches against His saints, nor even against men of the world.

Did we not know the corruption of our own hearts, it might not seem necessary to warn redeemed saints against the vice of using unclean language or relating salacious stories, but this is what is involved in the next expression, "filthy communication out of your mouth." Questionable stories and the relating of things true or false, the details of which only tend to feed a corrupt nature, these are to be shunned by a Christian. It was a wise answer and a deserved rebuke that a brother once gave to one in my own presence who began a story with the remark, "As there are no ladies here I want to tell you something I heard the other day." But the other checked him by saying, "Brother, though there are no ladies present, the Holy Spirit is here. Is your story fit for Him?" The first blushed in confusion and accepted the rebuke. We did not hear the story.

Were there any truth in the unscriptural theory held by some that the nature of the old man is eradicated in the case of a sanctified believer there would be no room whatsoever for the next injunction, "Lie not one to another, seeing that ye have put off the old man with his deeds." Lying is one of the very first evidences of the carnal nature. Of the wicked we read, "They go astray as soon as they are born, speaking lies." And untruthfulness is one of the hardest habits for anyone to overcome. It is so natural to these vain hearts of ours to try to make things appear better than they really are, to cover up our own failures and to accentuate the sins of others. Yet these are just different forms of lying, and we are called upon to judge all guile—untruthfulness of every character—in the light of the cross of Christ. The old man was judged there in the person of our Substitute, his deeds are to be refused, his habits put off as discarded garments that, as we have seen above, are in no sense fit for the new man.

In the next two verses we are told that we "have put on the new man, which is renewed in knowledge after the image of him that created him: where there is neither Greek nor Jew, circumcision nor uncircumcision, Barbarian, Scythian, bond nor free: but Christ is all, and in all." The new man, then, is the man in Christ, even as the old man was the man in Adam. This new man has a new, divinely imparted nature, and it is to this new nature God by the Spirit appeals. The new nature alone is capable of receiving divine instruction, and as the truth thus imparted controls the life, the believer manifests increasingly the image of Him who is the Head of the new creation. He Himself, as we have seen, is the image of the invisible God. Man was created in the image and likeness of God in the beginning, but that image became terribly marred through sin. In the new man this image again becomes manifest, and the very lineaments of Christ are seen in His people. This is true, no matter who or what they were before receiving the new life, whether cultured Greek or religious Jew; whether within the circle of the Abrahamic covenant marked off from the rest of humanity by the ordinance of circumcision, or whether in the world outside, strangers to the covenants of promise; whether barbarian or Scythian (that is, of the wild tribes outside the pale of civilization); whether slaves or free citizens. All alike were sinners; all alike are included in the term "the old man."

Now those who through grace have believed the gospel, from whichever of these classes they may have come, are members of the new creation and are seen by God as justified from all things and are possessors of a new and divine life. They belong to that new company where Christ is everything and in everyone. This is not to deny racial or class distinctions in the world—these the Christian must still recognize, and he has his responsibilities as to these distinctions—but above and beyond all these responsibilities is his new place in Christ, linked up with the new Head. It is from this that his new responsibilities flow; because he is a new creation man, he is called upon to manifest new ways and to put on new habits, new clothes suited to his new relationship. These new clothes will come before us in our next study.

In closing let me remark that new creation is not simply individual. It is not merely that I, as a believer, am a new creature in Christ Jesus. A better rendering of 2 Corinthians 5:17 would be, "Therefore if any man be in Christ, it is new creation: old things are passed away; behold, all things are become new."

> Joyful now the new creation
> Rests in undisturbed repose;
> Blest in Jesus' full salvation
> Sorrow now nor thraldom knows.

Not yet do we see the manifestation of all this, but "we see Jesus crowned with glory and honor," seated above all the changing scenes of time. Until He returns, it is as members of the new creation that we are called upon by our new ways to manifest the holiness, the grace, the righteousness, the love, and the compassion of Him who is "the beginning of the creation of God."

It is not that He is the first being created. This error was exposed in an earlier lecture. But He is the First, the Prince, the Head, the Origin of the new creation where all things are of God. "For in Christ Jesus neither circumcision availeth any thing, nor uncircumcision, but a new creature [or a new creation]. And as many as walk according to this rule [the rule, the controlling principle of this new creation], peace be on them and mercy, and upon the Israel of God" (Gal. 6:15–16). This is the very opposite of legality. It is the spontaneous expression of the life of the Head in the members here on earth!

CHAPTER 13

PRACTICAL HOLINESS BY CONFORMITY TO CHRIST IN RELATION TO OTHERS

Colossians 3:12–17

Put on therefore, as the elect of God, holy and beloved, bowels of mercies, kindness, humbleness of mind, meekness, longsuffering; forbearing one another, and forgiving one another, if any man have a quarrel against any: even as Christ forgave you, so also do ye. And above all these things put on charity, which is the bond of perfectness. And let the peace of God rule in your hearts, to the which also ye are called in one body; and be ye thankful. Let the word of Christ dwell in you richly in all wisdom; teaching and admonishing one another in psalms and hymns and spiritual songs, singing with grace in your hearts to the Lord. And whatsoever ye do in word or deed, do all in the name of the Lord Jesus, giving thanks to God and the Father by him. (vv. 12–17)

W e now come to consider our new clothes, the garments of the new man— these things that we are to put on in place of the old habits which have been discarded. It is a striking thing that both in the Scriptures and in our ordinary Anglo-Saxon speech we use at times the same words for clothing and behavior. We speak of a riding habit, a walking habit, habits of various descriptions, meaning of course, the clothing worn on particular occasions, and we may speak of our behavior as our habit. When in the Old Testament Solomon says, "Let thy garments be always white," we understand him, of course, to mean, let your habits or behavior be pure and righteous. The wicked are depicted as clothed with filthy garments, and self-righteousness is described as but filthy rags. The characteristics of the newborn man are garments of glory and beauty.

It is a common saying that you judge a man by his clothes. It is true that this is not always just. Many a princely character has, through poverty, been obliged to dress in worn and unbecoming garments, while rascals of the deepest dye have been arrayed like princes of the blood. But the same is true at times in regard to children of God and the unsaved. There are wolves who come in sheep's clothing, there are ministers of Satan who appear as ministers of righteousness, and, alas, there are real believers whose garments are often badly stained and rent by failure and sin. But, in the ordinary course of things, it is true that men are largely estimated according to their appearance, and Christians are expected to be adorned with good works and thus justify before men the profession they make of justification before God by faith in Jesus Christ. These are the two sides of truth emphasized by the apostle Paul in Romans and by James "the Lord's brother" in his intensely practical letter.

Let us see just what kind of habits or behavior should characterize the man in Christ, with what beautiful garments he should be arrayed. First of all we read, "Put on therefore, as the elect of God, holy and beloved, bowels of mercies." The elect of God are those whom He has foreknown from all eternity and who are manifest in time as believers in His Son. "Holy and beloved" is what they are as before God. They have been set apart in Christ. Sanctified by the blood of the everlasting covenant, they are dear to God because they are His own children, partakers of the divine nature. How unseemly if such are ever found stern and unfeeling toward others, recipients as they are of such grace themselves.

The ancients used the term *bowels* very much as we do the word *heart* to express the deepest feelings of humanity. We might read, "emotions of pity." While this may not be exactly a translation, it at least expresses in English the thought of the original. We are called upon to have hearts readily stirred to compassion and, like God Himself, delighting in mercy. Where it is otherwise, we may well question whether one has been born of God. Harshness in dealing with failing brethren, on the basis of the necessity of maintaining righteousness, is anything but the spirit of Christ. Yearning love that would lead us to go to any possible length without contravening God's righteous claims should ever characterize us in our dealings one with another. "Be pitiful," writes another apostle, and how much we need to take such an exhortation to heart. The cruelest things have been done in the name of Him who is the incarnation of infinite mercy. How He has been misrepresented in His attitude toward sin and sinners by many who profess to be His followers.

The next word is in keeping with this—*kindness*. It is quite impossible to maintain fellowship with God and not show the kindness of God toward others. There may indeed be a rigid, legal type of piety which leads one to imagine that he has been appointed of God to demonstrate His justice, but this is far from the godliness that is inculcated in the New Testament. Macaulay said of some of the sterner Puritans, "As one reads their writings he wonders if they had ever read a little volume called the New Testament." The loving-kindness of the Lord will be manifest in our kindness one to another. These two garments, emotions of pity and kindness are, we might say, inner vestments.

The next one is a cap for the head, *humbleness of mind*. Pride is of all things to God most hateful: "The proud he knoweth afar off." "Pride goeth before destruction, and an haughty spirit before a fall." The realization of one's own weakness and natural tendency to err will lead to low thoughts of self, and will make it easy to don the vesture of meekness. This is composed of rarer material than is often supposed. Our Lord was adorned with it. He could say, "I am meek and lowly in heart." How beautiful He appeared as thus arrayed. And Moses had a garment of this excellent texture, lawgiver though he was, for we read, "The man Moses was very meek, above all the men which were upon the face of the earth." But so rare is this grace that in the prophet Zephaniah, we are told to "seek meekness" (Zeph. 2:3), and this is after he has said, "Seek ye the LORD, all ye meek of the earth, which have wrought his judgment." So delicate is this fabric that it might readily wear away in the stress and strain of the trials of this life.

One needs therefore to be constantly in the presence of God seeking for this grace, which can be found nowhere else than in communion with Him. "Take my yoke upon you, and learn of me; for I am meek and lowly in heart" suggests the necessity of coming under His control if we would be adorned with meekness. The world will never understand the value of this lowly spirit. Our own lionhearted Theodore Roosevelt said once, "I hate a meek man." He probably did not realize that the boldest man, the most utterly unafraid man ever seen on earth, our Lord Jesus Christ, was in the fullest sense a meek man. Meekness is not inconsistent with bravery, and enables one to suffer and be strong when the world would "turn aside the way of the meek" (Amos 2:7).

Closely associated with meekness is the grace of "longsuffering," the readiness to endure grief suffering wrongfully. It is so natural for us when falsely accused to feel we must defend ourselves or to resent such treatment, but of our blessed Lord we read that when false witnesses had risen up against Him He answered not a word. When the adversary taunted King Hezekiah and his officers, charging them falsely and threatening severe treatment, the king's command to his people was, "Answer him not a word." God can be depended on to vindicate His own if they do not attempt to vindicate themselves, and so as they learn to commit their reputation, as well as all else that they once counted of value, to Christ Himself, they can patiently endure without resentment, praying for those who despitefully use them and who persecute them. In this they become consistent followers of the Man of Sorrows who could say, "They laid to my charge things I knew not."

We next read, "Forbearing one another, and forgiving one another, if any man have a quarrel against any: even as Christ forgave you, so also do ye." This is in exact accord with Ephesians 4:32: "And be ye kind one to another, tenderhearted, forgiving one another, even as God for Christ's sake (or, in Christ) hath forgiven you."

When teaching His disciples to pray our Lord told them to say, "Forgive us our trespasses as we forgive those who trespass against us," and He added, "When you stand praying, forgive: for if ye forgive not men their trespasses, neither will your heavenly Father forgive you" (author's translation). Some have thought the earlier passage is on lower ground than the later ones, but it does not seem necessary to put the one in any sense in opposition to the others. The forgiveness of which our Lord was speaking to His disciples was not the forgiveness of a sinner, but the forgiveness of a failing saint, one who could address God as "our Father," whereas the forgiveness spoken of here in Colossians and also in Ephesians is that of the sinner. Addressing His disciples our Lord says, as it were, "You are failing from day to day. You constantly need your Father's restorative and governmental forgiveness, and yet you cherish feelings of malice and enmity and an unforgiving spirit toward your brethren who offend you. If you do not forgive them you cannot expect your Father's forgiveness when you come to Him confessing your failures, and as long as this spirit of malice is cherished by you, you cannot really pray in faith."

Here Paul takes it up in another way. He says, as it were, "Think how freely you have been forgiven; think how much God has cast behind His back. In the light of this how can you hold hard feelings or maintain an unforgiving spirit toward those who have sinned against you? If God had dealt with you according to your offenses, how fearful would your judgment be, yet He in Christ has graciously forgiven all. He has put away every sin, thus making you fit for His holy presence. Your responsibility now is to forgive as you have been forgiven."

Some of you will remember the striking incident of the conversion of Macdonald Dubh, as narrated by Ralph Connor in "The Man from Glengarry." I understand the incident is not merely fiction, but is founded upon actual fact. The black Macdonald, a powerful, burly Highlander, living in Glengarry County, Ontario, had suffered untold anguish for years because of an injury inflicted upon him by a French Canadian some years before. He had nursed the desire to take a fearful vengeance upon his foe until it became a perfect obsession with him. Neither God nor eternity had any place in his life. It was in vain that the minister's wife tried to get him to forgive his enemy. She sought to have him repeat the Lord's Prayer, but he always balked at the words, "Forgive us our trespasses as we forgive those that trespass against us."

But God wrought in power in the Glengarry country, and there was a great revival, in which real Christians were aroused, and Christless men and women reached and saved. The black Macdonald heard the story of the cross told forth in living power in the Gaelic tongue, from the lips of the venerable Highland minister. It broke his heart and bowed him in penitence at the Savior's feet. When next the minister's wife went to visit him and tried to stress the necessity of forgiveness, he sobbed out, as he joined with her in what is generally called the Lord's Prayer, "*Oh, it's a little thing, it's a little thing, for I have been forgiven so much!*" It is this that grips the heart and enables one to bear in patience the ill-doing and evil-speaking of others and preserves from bitterness of spirit or any desire for vengeance. How can one, forgiven so much, ever hold an unforgiving spirit against any?

And now turn to verse 14 where we have the girdle that holds all our new garments in place. It might be rendered, "And over all these things put on love, which is the girdle of perfection." Just as the Oriental binds his flowing robes about him with a girdle, or sash, so the new man binds his new habits with the controlling power of love. Whatsoever is contrary to love is contrary to Christ. No amount of sophistical reasoning can make anything pleasing to God which is opposed to that divine love that He Himself sheds abroad in our hearts by the Holy Spirit, who is given unto us.

It would be well for some of us who are possessed with the idea that our great business on earth is to carry out what has sometimes been called Pauline truth, to remember that Pauline truth does not center in 1 Corinthians 5 but rises to its highest, experimentally, in 1 Corinthians 13. We are not to neglect the one in order to fulfill the other. Both are right and proper in their own places. In the portion we have been looking at we have had what should express our attitude toward our brethren in Christ and toward men of the world.

Now in verse 15 we get that which is distinctly personal: "Let the peace of God," or, as some manuscripts read, "the peace of Christ"—the same peace that ever filled His breast when here on earth. The peace that is His on the throne of God in heaven, where He sits far above all the storms of this lower scene—let that peace bear rule, or umpire, in your hearts. It is to this you are called in one body. We are to seek the things that make for peace as members of that body, and things whereby we may edify one another. But what is distinctly emphasized here is daily abiding in the blessedness of communion with our risen Lord, so that our hearts, like His own, may be kept in peace despite all we may be called upon to pass through, and thus we can fulfill the brief injunction, "Be ye thankful." Of the many sins of the unsaved not the least is unthankfulness. We are called upon to give thanks in every circumstance, "Giving thanks always for all things," knowing that nothing can ever enter into the life of the believer but what infinite love allows.

In the next two verses, which are very intimately linked with Ephesians 5:18–20, we read,

Let the word of Christ dwell in you richly in all wisdom; teaching and admonishing one another in psalms and hymns and spiritual songs, singing with grace in your hearts to the Lord. And whatsoever ye do in word or deed, do all in the name of the Lord Jesus, giving thanks to God and the Father by him.

As punctuated in the King James Version, verse 16 does not bring out the three admonitions clearly and distinctly, but as given above each one stands out separately and in its place. First we are told to let the word of Christ dwell in us richly. This is the only place in the New Testament where this particular expression, "the word of Christ," is found. It is most suggestive. The actual teaching of Christ, whether personally here on earth or by the Spirit since He has ascended to heaven, is to dwell in full measure in each believer. Thus equipped and controlled by the truth we will be able to bless and help others—in all wisdom teaching and admonishing one another. What we have is not given for ourselves alone. We are to be ready to communicate. Then, in the third place, as thus controlled by the Word of God, our lives will be lyrical and our hearts filled with melody, in psalms and hymns and spiritual songs, singing with grace in our hearts to the Lord. We read in Nehemiah, "The joy of the LORD is your strength." Holiness and happiness go together. Judah won a great victory when Jehoshaphat put the singers in the forefront of the army. Depend upon it, something is radically wrong with the Christian when he can no longer praise and rejoice.

Then, lastly, the entire life of the believer is summed up as subjection to the Lord. Whatsoever he does, whether in act or speech, all is to be in the name of the Lord Jesus, through whom he gives thanks to God, even the Father. There is no room whatsoever for self-will, for self-assertiveness here. As Christ in His humiliation could say, "I came . . . not to do mine own will, but the will of him that sent me," so the Christian, the new man, is left on earth to represent Christ, to do the will of the Lord and not to please himself.

By comparing the Ephesian passage with this it will become evident that we have the same results from being filled with the Spirit there, and filled with the Word here. A Word-filled Christian is a Spirit-filled Christian, that is, a Christian who is so controlled by the Word of God that it dominates his entire life and manifests that he is filled with the Holy Spirit. A careful consideration of these two passages might save from a great deal of fanaticism and misunderstanding in regard to the fullness of blessing that every truly converted soul cannot but crave.

CHAPTER 14

THE EARTHLY RELATIONSHIPS OF THE NEW MAN

Colossians 3:18–4:1

Wives, submit yourselves unto your own husbands, as it is fit in the Lord. Husbands, love your wives, and be not bitter against them. Children, obey your parents in all things: for this is well pleasing unto the Lord. Fathers, provoke not your children to anger, lest they be discouraged. Servants, obey in all things your masters according to the flesh; not with eyeservice, as menpleasers; but in singleness of heart, fearing God: and whatsoever ye do, do it heartily, as to the Lord, and not unto men; knowing that of the Lord ye shall receive the reward of the inheritance: for ye serve the Lord Christ. But he that doeth wrong shall receive for the wrong which he hath done: and there is no respect of persons. Masters, give unto your servants that which is just and equal; knowing that ye also have a Master in heaven. (3:18–4:1)

In these verses the Holy Spirit, who, as we have seen, is Himself not mentioned in this epistle save incidentally in verse 8 of chapter 1, gives us instruction in regard to the sanctification of the natural, or earthly, relationships of the new man. It would be a great mistake to suppose, as some have done, that because we are members of the new creation we need no longer consider ordinary human ties or responsibilities. While it is quite true that in the new creation there is neither male nor female, bond nor free, but all are one in Christ Jesus, it is important to remember that our bodies belong to the old creation still. It will not be until the redemption of the body at the coming of our Lord Jesus Christ and our gathering together unto Him that we shall be above the natural relationships in which we stand to one another as men and women here in the world.

Even in the church of God these human distinctions hold good as we are reminded in the epistles to the Corinthians and to Timothy and Titus. To say as some do that because there is neither male nor female in the new creation, we are to pay no attention to the divinely given order pertaining to the respective places of man and woman in the church of God on earth is not only to go beyond Scripture but is positive disobedience to the Word of God. As long as we are subject to human limitations, so long must we recognize our human responsibilities and seek to maintain these in a scriptural way in order that we may commend the gospel of Christ.

There is no condition in which the new life is more blessedly manifested than in circumstances sometimes hard for flesh and blood to endure, but where grace enables, brings triumph. A comparison of the instruction given in Colossians in the verses quoted above, with similar instruction in the epistle to the Ephesians, will show us that the apostle deals very briefly here with what he has taken up at much greater length there. The one epistle should be compared with the other, and both with similar teaching given in 1 Peter, in order that we may get the mind of God as fully revealed in regard to the great and important principles that govern our behavior.

It will be noticed that in each of the Scripture passages referred to the weaker is dealt with first, and then the stronger; or the one subject first, and then the one in authority. So here we have wives and husbands, then children and fathers, and lastly, servants and masters. Let us examine with some degree of care what the Holy Spirit says to each one.

"Wives, submit yourselves unto your own husbands, as it is fit in the Lord." Where husband and wife are both Christians seeking to do the will of God, in whose hearts there is real mutual affection and esteem, there will be no difficulty whatsoever in regard to such an admonition as this. But it will require true grace to yield loving obedience when perhaps the husband is a carnal, worldly, and unreasonable man. Yet we need to remember the marriage relationship is divinely ordained, and as the old wedding ceremony puts it, "not to be lightly entered into" and according to the Word of God not easily to be terminated. "For better, for worse, until death do us part," are words often flippantly uttered with no real conception of their seriousness.

For the Christian woman this relationship once entered into there is no other position in conformity with the will of God than that of godly submission to the husband whom she herself has chosen. The present loose ideas in regard to easy divorce are bearing fearful fruit which will increase unto more ungodliness as the end draws near, until there will be duplicated in Christendom the corruption and vileness of the days before the flood and the unspeakable immoralities of the cities of the plain. Of all this our blessed Lord has warned us most solemnly. For one to seek to dissolve the marriage relationship because of incompatibility of temperament is to fly in the face of the Word of the living God. Death, or what is equivalent to it, the infidelity of husband or wife, is the only scriptural ground for termination of the marriage contract, leaving the other party free to remarry.

It is true that 1 Corinthians 7:11 would imply that there may be circumstances in which no self-respecting woman could continue to live in this relationship, because of unspeakable cruelty or abominable conditions which would be ruinous to soul and body alike. But if she departs she is to remain unmarried, and if conditions change, she may be reconciled to her husband. But so long as she remains with him she is responsible to recognize his headship as the one appointed by God to provide for the family, and even though conditions may sometimes be very distressing, she is to seek to win her wayward spouse by manifesting the grace of Christ.

"As it is fit in the Lord," suggests that gracious demeanor which ever characterized Him while He was in this scene, and also that her submission and obedience will never be such as to injure conscience or dishonor the Lord. In this she must act as before God, for after all, hers is the submission of a wife and not of a slave. It is loyalty to him who is her head that is enjoined.

In verse 19 we read, "Husbands, love your wives, and be not bitter against them." And, right here, how many husbands fail! Imperiously demanding submission from the wife, how little do they show the love of Christ in their dealings with those thus dependent upon them! The Christian husband is to accept his place of headship as a sacred responsibility put upon him by God Himself and is to exercise his authority for the blessing of his home in the love of Christ. And just as some wives may be united to tyrannical and unreasonable men, so there are husbands who, after marriage, find that one who in days of courtship seemed so docile and affectionate is a veritable termagant and as unreasonable as it is possible to be. But still the husband is to love and care for her, showing all consideration, "giving honour unto the wife, as unto the weaker vessel," as Peter puts it, without indulging in wrath or anger. How much is involved in the exhortation, "Be not bitter against them." God knew how petty and trying some women's ways would be when He said to good men, "Be not bitter against them." In the power of the new life one may manifest patience and grace under the most trying circumstances.

Now we come to the injunction to children: "Children, obey your parents in all things: for this is well pleasing unto the Lord." In childhood days parents stand in relation to their children as God Himself in relation to the parent. Children who do not obey their parents when young will not obey God when older. The natural heart is ever rebellious against authority, and perhaps never more strikingly has this been manifested than in these democratic days in which we live. But Christian children should be examples of godly submission to father and mother or whoever may be in authority over them, and parents are responsible to instill into their hearts the divine requirement of obedience. For young people professing piety, to ignore this principle of obedience is to manifest utter insubjection to the One they own as Lord.

But again we notice how carefully the Spirit of God guards all this when He says, "Fathers, provoke not your children to anger, lest they be discouraged." Parental rule may be of such a character as to fill the growing boy or girl with indignation and contempt instead of drawing out the young heart in love and obedience. How easy it is, when come to manhood, to forget the feelings of a child, and so to implant in the hearts of the little ones resentment instead of tender affection. Surely this is contrary to every instinct of the new man. The Christian father is to imitate Him who is our Father-God.

It is when He addresses the servants that he goes into the greatest details. These, in the days when this epistle was written, were slaves and not free men who served for wages, but if such instruction as we have here was applicable to bondmen, how much more does it apply to those who have the privilege of selling their services and of terminating engagements at will. There is no excuse whatsoever for surly, dishonest service because perhaps the master or mistress may be exasperating and unappreciative. Notice the exhortation, "Servants, obey in all things your masters according to the flesh; not with eyeservice, as menpleasers; but in singleness of heart, fearing God." How this glorifies the servant's lowly path in whatsoever capacity he is called upon to labor for others. He is privileged to look at all his service as done unto the Lord Himself.

Thus he labors faithfully, not only under the master's eye, but when unseen by man. He carries on his appointed task conscientiously in singleness of heart, having the fear of God before his soul, according as it is written, "And whatsoever ye do, do it heartily, as to the Lord, and not unto men: knowing that of the Lord ye shall receive the reward of the inheritance: [because] ye serve the Lord Christ."

What a cheer was this to the Roman or Grecian slave, toiling on day after day with the most faithful ministrations taken perhaps but as a matter of course. Yet if all were done as to the Lord one could be sure that in the coming day, the day of manifestation, He Himself would reward accordingly, accepting all the service as done unto Him. On the other hand, if treated cruelly, and perhaps overreached and cheated out of the due reward of his labor, the Christian servant does well to remember that God is taking note of all, and a day is coming when every wrong will be put right. Things that can never be settled here in righteousness will have a full settlement then, for, "He that doeth wrong shall receive for the wrong which he hath done: and there is no respect of persons." Whether it be the servant who is unfaithful or the master who is unappreciative, the Lord Himself will bring everything to light at His judgment seat, or in the case of the unsaved, at the Great White Throne, when every man shall be judged according to his works.

It is unfortunate that the chapter break comes just where it does. It would seem far more suitable to close chapter 3 with the next verse, and let chapter 4 begin with verse 2, for it is evident that verse 1 concludes this particular section. It is a message to those in authority: "Masters, give unto your servants that which is just and equal; knowing that ye also have a Master in heaven." In every instance it is to the new man He speaks. Ungodly masters could not be expected to take heed to such an admonition as this, but it is addressed to one who, while master in his relationship to his servants, is himself but a servant to his own Master in heaven. He may well give heed to what is here so impressively urged upon him. He is to treat his servants as he would have the Lord treat him. He is to be characterized by fairness, giving to those beneath him that which is just and equal, knowing that all the time his heavenly Master is looking on. When he comes to give account of his service, his relations to those who on earth served under him will all be carefully gone into, when everything will be brought to light.

What marvelous principles are these which we have seen so simply stated. Only one who knows something of the conditions prevailing in the Roman Empire at the time this letter was written can realize how revolutionary they were. In those days, wives, children, and slaves had practically no standing before the law, except as husbands, fathers, or masters might desire to recognize them. But this glorious truth of the new man, this blessed unfolding of the new creation, tinged with glory every earthly relationship in which the Christian was found. It is like the blue border upon the hem of the pious Israelite's garment. Even on the lower edge where that long flowing robe came most nearly in contact with the earth, this ribbon of blue was seen. Blue, as we well know, is the heavenly color. The Israelite was to look upon it and remember that he had owned the Lord to be his God, He who had said, "Be ye holy; for I am holy." As he looked upon the ribbon of blue he was to remember his responsibility to honor and to glorify the God of heaven in his life on the earth. We as Christians are to manifest the heavenly character in every lawful relationship which God has established during the present order of things for the blessing of mankind.

There is a story told of one of the Dauphins of France who had an English tutor. This teacher found his princely pupil very difficult to handle. Proud and haughty, and impatient of restraint, the young man submitted unwillingly to schoolroom restrictions and his foreign instructor was often at his wits' end how to deal with him. One morning as his pupil came to him, the tutor placed upon the lapel of his jacket a purple rosette, saying to him, "This is the royal color. As you wear it I want you to remember that you are the Crown Prince of France, and that it is incumbent upon you ever to behave in a princely way. If you are willful or disobedient I shall, of course, not attempt to punish you, as that is not in my province. But I shall simply point to the purple, and you will understand what I mean, that I do not feel your behavior is worthy of a princely lad." The appeal to the purple! How striking the suggestion. May we not say that to us there is a similar appeal, but, to use the Old Testament picture, it is the appeal to the blue! Wives, husbands, children, fathers, masters, and servants, are all alike called upon to manifest the holiness of heaven, to display the heavenly character, even in earthly relationships.

It is in just such things as these that the power of the new life is wonderfully manifested. "Holding the Head" is not merely maintaining ecclesiastical truth, but it is shown forth in a holy, godly life—in subjection of heart and mind to Christ, and never more fully than in the way we live in the family, and in connection with business and social responsibilities.

CHAPTER 15

Concluding Exhortations

Colossians 4:2–6

Continue in prayer, and watch in the same with thanksgiving; withal praying also for us, that God would open unto us a door of utterance, to speak the mystery of Christ, for which I am also in bonds: that I may make it manifest, as I ought to speak. Walk in wisdom toward them that are without, redeeming the time. Let your speech be always with grace, seasoned with salt, that ye may know how ye ought to answer every man. (vv. 2–6)

One of the most common sins among Christians today is that of prayerlessness. No doubt this has been true throughout the centuries. And yet we are again and again not only exhorted, but distinctly commanded, to pray.

- "Men ought always to pray, and not to faint."
- "Pray without ceasing."
- "Praying always with all prayer and supplication in the Spirit."
- "Praying in the Holy Ghost."

To these might be added many similar expressions, reminding us that prayer is in very truth "the Christian's vital breath." It is the life of the new man. One can no more have a happy, triumphant Christian experience who neglects this spiritual exercise than one can be well and strong physically who shuts himself up in a close room to which the sun never penetrates and where pure air is unknown. The soul flourishes in an atmosphere of prayer.

And yet the Christian has sometimes been asked, "Why do we need to pray? If God is infinitely wise and infinitely good, as the Holy Scriptures declare Him to be, why need any of His creatures petition Him regarding anything which they conceive to be either for their own good or for the blessing of others? Is it not a higher and purer faith that leads one to ignore these exercises altogether and simply to trust Him to do what He sees to be best in every circumstance?" Those who reason thus manifest but little acquaintance with the Word of God, and little realize the needs of the soul.

Prayer is, first of all, communion with God. Our blessed Lord Himself, in the days of His flesh, is seen again and again leaving the company of His disciples and going out into some desert place on a mountainside or into a garden that His spirit might be refreshed as He bowed in prayer alone with the Father. From such reasons of fellowship He returned to do His mightiest works and to bear witness to the truth. And in this He is our great Exemplar. We need to pray as much as we need to breathe. Our souls will languish without it, and our testimony will be utterly fruitless if we neglect it.

We are told to continue in prayer. This does not mean that we are to be constantly teasing God in order that we may obtain what we might think would add most to our happiness or be best for us, but we are to abide in a sense of His presence and of our dependence upon His bounty. We are to learn to talk to Him and to quietly wait before Him, too, in order that we may hear His voice as He speaks to us. We are bidden to bring everything to Him in prayer, assured that if we ask anything according to His will He hears us. But because we are so ignorant and so shortsighted we need ever to remember that we are to leave the final disposal of things with Him who makes no mistakes. Without anxiety as to anything, we may bring everything to Him in prayer and supplication with thanksgiving, making known our requests in childlike simplicity. Then, leaving all in His hands, we go forth in fullest confidence as our hearts say, "Thy will be done," knowing that He will do for us exceeding abundantly above all that we ask or think.

We need to be often reminded that we cannot pray as we should unless we are careful as to our walk before God, and so we are told not only to continue in prayer but to watch in the same, and that with thanksgiving. "Watch and pray." Here are two things that must never be separated. It is so easy to slip into a careless condition of soul, to become entangled amid worldly and unholy snares, so that we lose all spiritual discernment and our prayers become selfish. When this is the case, it is vain to think that we shall obtain anything from the Lord. But where there is watchfulness and sobriety, with honest confession and self-judgment when we realize failure has come in, we can pray in fullest confidence, knowing that all hindrance is removed.

Here, as in Philippians 4, we are reminded that thanksgiving for past mercies should accompany prayer for present and future blessing. To receive God's good gifts as a mere matter of course soon dries up spiritual affection, and we become self-centered instead of Christ-centered and foolishly imagine that God is in some way bound to lavish His mercies upon us whether we are grateful or not. In our dealings with one another we feel it keenly if ingratitude is manifested and kindness goes unacknowledged. Even though we may give unselfishly we like appreciation, and a hearty "thank you" makes one all the more ready to minister again where there is need. And we may be assured that our God finds joy in His people's praises. He loves to give, but He delights in our appreciation of His benefits.

Paul, unquestionably the greatest preacher and teacher that the Christian dispensation has known, was not above requesting the prayers of the people of God. He felt his need of their prayer help, and so he says, "Withal praying also for us, that God would open unto us a door of utterance, to speak the mystery of Christ, for which I am also in bonds: that I may make it manifest, as I ought to speak." He did not feel that because he was in prison his work was over. Although unable to face the multitudes in public places as in past years, he was ever on the lookout for opportunities of service, and he would have the saints join with him in prayer that even in his prison cell a door of utterance might be open to him. How natural it would have been for him to give up in despair and settle down in utter discouragement, or simply to endure passively the long, weary months of imprisonment, taking it for granted that nothing could really be accomplished for God so far as gospel fruit was concerned until he should be free. But he was of another mind entirely. His circumstances did not indicate that God had forsaken him nor that He had set him to one side. He was eagerly looking for fresh opportunities to advance upon the enemy.

We are told that just before the first battle of the Marne in the World War of 1914–1918, Marshal Foch, the great French general, reported: "My centre is giving; my left wing is retreating; the situation is excellent; I am attacking." This was not mere military bombast, for the marshal realized that apparent defeat could be turned into victory by acting with resolution and alacrity at the very moment when the enemy seemed to be triumphant.

Doubtless the Devil thought he had gained a great advantage when he shut Paul up in prison, but from that prison cell came at least four of the great church epistles and some of the pastoral letters, which have been the means of untold blessing to millions throughout the centuries. And from that cell, too, the gospel went out. First to the prison guards and through them to many more in Caesar's palace who might not otherwise have been reached. How important it is not to give ground to Satan, but in prayer and faith to turn every defeat into a victory by seizing the opportunity and advancing against the foe, assured that our great Captain knows no retreat.

Alas, we spend so much time halting between two opinions, debating what we should do, and doing nothing. We need the grace of decision that will enable us to seize the opportune moment and act upon it in the fear of God. And this is emphasized in the verse that follows: "Walk in wisdom toward them that are without, redeeming the time." In our relationships with men of the world, how we need to remember that opportunities to warn of judgment to come and to point them to Christ once given may never come again. Therefore, the tremendous importance of buying up such privileges of service in the light of the judgment seat of Christ.

The day of grace is fast passing away. We meet men once, perhaps, never to see them again. While it is perfectly true that we cannot be forever pestering people about what they would call our religious notions, yet it is the part of wisdom to be on the lookout for every opening that will give us the privilege to minister Christ to their souls.

> To each man's life there comes a time supreme,
>   One day, one night, one morning or one noon,
>   One freighted hour, one moment opportune,
> One rift through which sublime fulfillments gleam,
> One space when faith goes tiding with the stream,
>   One Once in balance 'twixt Too Late, Too Soon,
>   And ready for the passing instant's boon
> To tip in favor of uncertain beam.
>
> Ah, happy he who, knowing how to wait,
>   Knows, also how to watch, and work, and stand,

On Life's broad deck alert, and at the prow
To seize the passing moment, big with fate,
    From Opportunity's extended hand,
When the great clock of Destiny strikes NOW!

But if we would witness to the Lord in such a way that our testimony will really count we must be careful that our walk agrees with our speech. Careless behavior when in the company of worldlings will only make them feel that we do not ourselves believe the tremendous truths which we would press upon them. How careful preachers need to be in regard to this! The world is so quick to judge and will only turn away with disgust from a man who is serious on the platform but frivolous among men. He who is solemn as he preaches of divine realities but is a giggling buffoon when out in company need not think that he will make any permanent impression for good upon the hearts and consciences of those among whom he mingles. Many a servant of Christ in his anxiety to be accepted of men and to become what is called today "a good mixer," sincerely hoping thereby to commend his message, has found to his sorrow that he has paid too high a price for his popularity. He has but cheapened himself and his ministry by coming down to the level of natural men who know not the power of the new life.

I remember well a friend speaking once of two preachers. One was perhaps a bit unduly serious, not that anyone can be too sober as he faces the realities of eternity, but the man in question was perhaps a bit too stern to readily make friends among those whom he wished to help. The other was the very soul of cordiality. He would tell a good story, smoke a good cigar, and make himself hail-fellow-well-met with all and sundry with whom he came in contact. Speaking of him my friend said, "Dr. Blank is a fine fellow. I do enjoy an hour in his company. He makes me forget all my troubles, but," he added thoughtfully, "if I were dying I'd rather have Mr. So-and-So come and pray with me."

Ah, my brethren, let us not forfeit our high and holy calling as Christ's representatives in order that we may obtain popularity among men who have little relish for divine things. This does not mean that we are called upon to be disagreeable in our behavior or conversation, for we are told, "Let your speech be alway with grace, seasoned with salt, that ye may know how ye ought to answer every man." Gracious speech flows from a heart established in the grace of God. Of Jesus the psalmist wrote, "Grace is poured into Thy lips." He could say, "Thy gentleness hath made me great." But this did not make Him indifferent to evil nor unfaithful in dealing with those who needed rebuke.

"Seasoned with salt" suggests the preservative power of faithfulness. There is always a danger that a gracious man will become a weak man and will lack courage to speak out faithfully when occasion demands it. In the law it is written, "Thou shalt in any wise rebuke thy neighbour, [thou shalt] not suffer sin upon him." We are all our brothers' keepers to a certain extent. While nothing is more contrary to the spirit of Christ than an overweening, captious, fault-finding spirit, yet where Christ's honor is at stake, or where we realize a brother is standing in dangerous places, we need the salt of righteousness to season gracious speech in order that we may know how to speak to every man.

And if we would perfect ourselves in this grace we need to live more in company with the Lord Jesus Christ Himself. Follow Him through the Gospels in His wondrous ministry of grace and truth here on earth. See how marvelously He met each individual case. F. W. Grant has well said, "Our Lord had no stereotyped method of dealing with souls." He took up each case on its merits. He did not talk to the woman at the well in the same way He addressed Nicodemus, the ruler of the Jews. He probed the depths of each heart and ministered according to the need.

Jesus' devoted follower, the apostle Paul, the author of this divinely inspired letter to the Colossians, was ever exercised in regard to the same thing. He was "made all things to all men if by any means he might save some" (author's translation). In the Jewish synagogue he reasoned out the Scriptures like the most able rabbi or doctor of the law. When he stood on Mars Hill among the Athenian philosophers he was a master of rhetoric and showed full acquaintance with Greek thought and literature. But he spoke "not as pleasing men, but God, which trieth [the] hearts," until his great address was interrupted by the excited throng about him, who spurned the idea of the resurrection of the body. Addressing the idolaters of Lycaonia he met them on their own ground and appealed from nature to nature's God, seeking to turn them from their vanities and draw their hearts to the Creator of all things. How different in all this was both the Master and the servant to many who today seem to pride themselves on their outspokenness and indifference to the views and opinions of others.

Is it any wonder that men turn from them in disgust and refuse to listen to what seems to them but the dogmatic utterances of self-centered egotists. On the other hand, as intimated above, there are those who seek to be gracious but who utterly lack faithfulness, and who would gloss over any doctrine or evil in the lives of their hearers rather than run the risk of giving offense. How much divine wisdom is needed, and how close must the servant keep to the Master Himself in order that he may know how to answer every man.

CHAPTER 16

CLOSING SALUTATIONS

Colossians 4:7–18

All my state shall Tychicus declare unto you, who is a beloved brother, and a faithful minister and fellowservant in the Lord: whom I have sent unto you for the same purpose, that he might know your estate, and comfort your hearts; with Onesimus, a faithful and beloved brother, who is one of you. They shall make known unto you all things which are done here. Aristarchus my fellowprisoner saluteth you, and Marcus, sister's son to Barnabas, (touching whom ye received commandments: if he come unto you, receive him;) and Jesus, which is called Justus, who are of the circumcision. These only are my fellowworkers unto the kingdom of God, which have been a comfort unto me. Epaphras, who is one of you, a servant of Christ, saluteth you, always labouring fervently for you in prayers, that ye may stand perfect and complete in all the will of God. For I bear him record, that he hath a great zeal for you, and them that are in Laodicea, and them in Hierapolis. Luke, the beloved physician, and Demas, greet you. Salute the brethren which are in Laodicea, and Nymphas, and the church which is in his house. And when this epistle is read among you, cause that it be read also in the church of the

Laodiceans; and that ye likewise read the epistle from Laodicea. And say to Archippus, Take heed to the ministry which thou hast received in the Lord, that thou fulfil it. The salutation by the hand of me Paul. Remember my bonds. Grace be with you. Amen. (vv. 7–18)

This last section, though somewhat lengthy, does not require very much in the way of either exposition or explanation. It is interesting, however, to compare the references to the same person mentioned here with those in other epistles.

We do not know much about Tychicus, mentioned in verse 7, excepting that in Ephesians 6:21–22 he is again spoken of in almost the same terms. It is evident that he was one in whom the apostle had implicit confidence. He speaks of him in each passage as a beloved brother and faithful minister, adding here a third expression—"fellow servant in the Lord." Beloved and yet faithful! What a rare but blessed combination is this!

So often men who seek to be faithful become almost unconsciously stern and ungracious, thereby forfeiting the tender affection of the people of God, even though they may be looked upon with respect as men of principle who can be depended upon to do and say the righteous thing at all cost to themselves or others. Unhappily, in the last instance, they may manifest very little real concern for the peace of mind or comfort of heart of those who disagree with them. On the other hand, many a beloved brother purchases the affectionate regard of the saints at the cost of faithfulness to truth. It is far better to be true to Christ and His Word, and thus have His approval, than to be approved of men and loved because of weakness in enforcing what is according to truth.

Tychicus evidently went to neither extreme. He was undoubtedly a lovable man because of his gracious demeanor and his tender solicitude for the welfare of the saints, but at the same time he was faithful in ministering the Word of God, rebuking iniquity and also comforting the penitent. Such men are rarer than we realize. In them we see the delightful combination of the shepherd's heart and the prophet's spirit. One cannot but think how alike in character were Timothy and Tychicus. Both were loyal to the Word of God, and both sought the comfort and blessing of the people of God.

In verse 9 Onesimus is spoken of in similar terms. He is called a "faithful and beloved brother." It is evident that he did not have the gift that marked Tychicus, but the two characteristics we have noticed were manifest in him. We know much more of his history than of several others mentioned in this chapter. The brief letter to Philemon tells us a great deal regarding him. He had been a dishonest runaway slave. He had robbed his master and apparently wasted his ill-gotten gains before he was brought to Christ through coming in contact with Paul in Rome. Philemon himself had been converted through the same devoted servant, so we may see, in mercy being extended to the thieving slave, a wondrous picture of sovereign grace.

> Sov'reign grace o'er sin abounding;
>   Ransomed souls the tidings swell!
> 'Tis a deep that knows no sounding;
>   Who its length and breadth can tell?
>   On its glories
>   Let my soul forever dwell.

After Onesimus was brought to Christ, Paul sent him back to his master, offering himself to become his surety in the tender words, "If thou count me therefore a partner, receive him as myself. If he hath wronged thee, or oweth thee ought, put that to my account; I Paul have written it with mine own hand, I will repay it." What a gospel picture is this! It is Christ Himself who has assumed the responsibilities of the penitent sinner. "We are all God's Onesimuses," said Luther. Christ paid our debt that we might be accepted in Him before God.

> He bore on the tree, the sentence for me,
> And now both the Surety and sinner are free.

And when thus redeemed, it is our happy privilege to serve Him in glorious liberty and say with the psalmist, "Truly I am thy servant; . . . thou hast loosed my bonds."

Of Aristarchus, whom Paul here calls his fellow prisoner, we read in Acts 19 that he was a Macedonian traveling with Paul and endangered his very life on behalf of the gospel at the time of the uproar in Ephesus. He is also mentioned again in Philemon 24 as a fellow laborer with the apostle. His name would imply that he was of the so-called upper classes, an aristocrat of Macedonia, who for the sake of the kingdom of God had renounced his place of prominence in the world to become a bondman of Jesus Christ.

We are glad to see the affectionate way in which Paul here writes of Marcus, the nephew of Barnabas. Years before, this young man had been the cause of serious contention between these two devoted men of God. Paul had lost confidence in John Mark because of his leaving the work and returning to his mother in Jerusalem upon the completion of the evangelistic tour in Cyprus. Barnabas, kindly in spirit and evidently moved by natural affection, wanted to give the unfaithful helper a second chance, but Paul was obdurate. He felt he could not afford to jeopardize the success of their work by again taking with them one who had proved himself a weakling. Which one really had the mind of God, we are not told. But we are thankful indeed to find that Mark "made good," as we say, and became a trusted and honored man of God, companion to Peter (see 1 Peter 5:13), and dear to Paul as well as to his uncle Barnabas. He is again mentioned in Philemon 24 as a fellow laborer, and Paul requests Timothy to bring Mark with him, in 2 Timothy 4:11. The fact that he needed the spiritual commendation of verse 10 would seem to imply that at the time of writing there were some who still stood in doubt of him, but the apostle's recommendation would remove all that.

The next name, "Jesus, which is called Justus," might well remind us of the humiliation to which our blessed Lord stooped in grace when He became a man in order to give His life for sinners. To us there is only one *Jesus*. That name is now above every name and shines resplendent in highest glory, unique and precious, a name with which none other can ever be compared. But we need to be reminded that *Jesus* represents the Hebrew name *Joshua* and was in common use when our Lord was here on earth. And so we have here a brother otherwise unknown bearing the same name as his Savior, and not only that but surnamed The Just. This latter title was given to men because of their recognized integrity as in the case of Joseph Barsabas of Acts 1:23 and an otherwise unknown Justus in Acts 18:7.

There is something peculiarly suggestive in the way the apostle eulogizes these brethren whose salutations he thus conveys to the Colossians. "These only are my fellowworkers unto the kingdom of God, which have been a comfort unto me." It is evident that then, as now, gift and grace did not necessarily go together. There were others who were perhaps energetic enough in service but who were anything but brotherly in their attitude toward Paul.

Of Epaphras we have already had the apostle's estimate in 1:7. Here he draws special attention to this man's fervency in prayer. It was he who had come from Colosse to visit Paul and to acquaint him with the conditions that called forth this letter. That he had some ability as a preacher and teacher we know, for it was through his ministry these Colossians had been won to Christ and the assembly formed there. But his greatest ministry was evidently one of prayer. In that he labored fervently, striving earnestly in supplication before God, so deeply concerned was he for the saints that they might enter into the truth in all its fullness and thus in practical experience stand as full-grown and filled full, or complete, in all the will of God. In this prayer Paul joined, as we have seen in 1:9. This earnest apostle of prayer, Epaphras, had not confined his ministry or interest to Colosse, but he bore in his heart, in the same intense zeal, the neighboring assemblies of Laodicea and Hierapolis.

It is most pathetic to compare verse 14 with 2 Timothy 4:10–11. Here we read, "Luke, the beloved physician, and Demas, greet you." But in writing to Timothy the apostle says, "Demas hath forsaken me, having loved this present world, and [hath] departed unto Thessalonica. . . . Only Luke is with me." From the day he joined Paul's company (as intimated in Acts 16 where the change of the pronoun from "they" to "us" showed that Luke formed one of the party at Troas, vv. 8–9), "Luke, the beloved physician," was one of Paul's most devoted helpers. He remained with him to the end and possibly saw him martyred.

Demas and Luke seem to have been intimately associated, for both here and in Philemon 24 the two names are found together, but upon the occasion of Paul's second imprisonment we learn that the love of the world had been too much for Demas. He found the itinerant preacher's lot too hard, and he left the apostle in his hour of need and went off to Thessalonica. There is no hint that he plunged into a life of sin. He may have gone into some respectable business, but the Holy Spirit relentlessly exposes the hidden springs of his changed behavior. He loved this present world. No longer are he and Luke joined in devoted service. Demas had chosen an easier path.

Salutations are sent to the Laodicean brethren, and Nymphas, who was evidently prominent among them and in whose house they met for worship, is especially mentioned. We may gather from verse 16 how the apostolic letters were early circulated among the churches. This Colossian epistle was not only to be read locally but was to be read also in the assembly of the Laodiceans. And a letter sent to the latter church was to be sent on to Colosse. This epistle from Laodicea (observe not *to* Laodicea) is probably our epistle to the Ephesians, and is generally regarded as a circular letter that went first to Ephesus and then to other churches in the Roman proconsular province of Asia, thus reaching Colosse from Laodicea. We have already seen how important it is to study the two together as they are divinely linked in such a wonderful way.

In verse 17 Paul gives a special admonition to Archippus, also mentioned in the letter to Philemon, who was apparently a servant of Christ ministering the Word at Colosse but had a tendency not uncommon in some young preachers to settle down comfortably and take things easily. To him the apostle sends the message, "Take heed to the ministry which thou hast received in the Lord, that thou fulfil it." Promptness and energy are as important in spiritual service as in anything else.

There is an incident related in connection with two leading generals of the Southern Confederacy of America that might well speak to every servant of Christ. General Robert E. Lee once sent word to General Stonewall Jackson that he would be glad to talk with him at his convenience on some matter of no great urgency. General Jackson instantly rode to Headquarters, through most inclement weather. When General Lee expressed surprise at seeing him, Jackson exclaimed, "General Lee's slightest wish is a supreme command to me, and I always take pleasure in prompt obedience." It is to be hoped that this same spirit laid hold of Archippus, and that he profited by the prodding of the aged apostle.

The epistle was signed in accordance with Paul's usual custom with his own hand. According to the note at the end, Tychicus and Onesimus acted as his amanuenses in producing this letter, but he appended his signature. How much would one give to have an autographed copy of this or any other of his letters! He would have them remember his bonds both as stirring them up to prayer and to remind them that the servant's path is one of suffering and rejection.

He closes with the customary benediction, "Grace be with you. Amen." This is not so full as that in the last verse of 2 Thessalonians, which he tells us is the token of genuineness in every epistle of his. But as we go over all the thirteen letters that bear his name and the anonymous letter to the Hebrews we see that in every one there is some message about grace at the end. He was preeminently the apostle of grace, and it is no matter of surprise that this precious word should be his secret mark, as it were, thus authenticating every letter. May that grace abound in us as it already has abounded toward us through the abundant mercy of our God.

> Grace is the sweetest sound
> That ever reached our ears,
> When conscience charged and Justice frowned,
> 'Twas grace removed our fears!

We began with grace, we are kept by grace, and it is grace that will bring us home at last.

NOTES

PHILIPPIANS
Chapter 14: Self-Confidence Set Aside for Christ

1. Does not the expression imply, however, that Saul had fought against the testimonies to his conscience?—such as Stephen's, whose face they saw "shining as an angel's" while testifying before the council of the Jews, yet to whose death Saul gave his vote, keeping the garments of those that stoned him. And how many other appeals to his conscience, if not to his heart, there must have been as he beat and dragged men and women to prison, compelling them to blaspheme Jesus, if possible! (Editor)

Chapter 15: Paul's Steadfast Purpose

1. If any are perplexed as to this, may I recommend C. H. Mackintosh, *The Two Resurrections, and the Judgment* (New York: Loizeaux, n.d.).

COLOSSIANS
Chapter 5: Paul's Twofold Ministry

1. For fuller discussion of this interesting subject the inquiring or studious reader is referred to the author's handbook titled "The Mysteries of God."